HOW TO COOK
LIKE A MAN

HOW TO COOK LIKE A MAN

A MEMOIR OF COOKBOOK OBSESSION

DANIEL DUANE

B L O O M S B U R Y
NEW YORK • LONDON • NEW DELHI • SYDNEY

Parts of this book appeared first, in substantially different form, in *Men's Journal*, the *New York Times Magazine*, *Food & Wine*, *Bon Appétit*, and *Sierra*.

Published by Bloomsbury USA, New York

All papers used by Bloomsbury USA are natural, recyclable products made from wood grown in well-managed forests. The manufacturing processes conform to the environmental regulations of the country of origin.

LIBRARY OF CONGRESS CATALOGING–IN–PUBLICATION DATA
HAS BEEN APPLIED FOR.

ISBN: 978-1-60819-102-4 (hardback)

First published by Bloomsbury USA in 2012
This paperback edition published in 2013

Paperback ISBN: 978-1-62040-066-1

1 3 5 7 9 10 8 6 4 2

Typeset by Westchester Book Group
Printed and bound in the U.S.A. by Thomson-Shore Inc., Dexter, Michigan

For Liz, Hannah, and Audrey

The stove, the bins, the cupboards, I had learned forever, make an inviolable throne room. From them I ruled; temporarily I controlled. I felt powerful, and I loved that feeling.

—M. F. K. Fisher, *The Gastronomical Me*

MENU

Preface: A Man's Place Is in the Kitchen   xi

Part One: The Burrito Years

1. You Are the Way You Eat   3
2. On the Cookbook as Scripture   18

Part Two: The Alice Years

3. Recipes Are for Idiots Like Me   35
4. We All Need Something to Believe In   50
5. What French Women Can Teach Us   63
6. The Happy Hunting Ground   75
7. On the Role of the Menu in Human Affairs   84

Part Three: What Is Cooking For?

8. The Meat Period in Every Man's Life   105
9. My Kung Fu Is Not Strong   119
10. On Cooking and Carpentry   134

CONTENTS

11. Gluttony as Heroism   153

12. Recipes Are for Idiots Like Me, Take Two   179

13. What We Talk About When We Talk About
     Our Last Supper   195

Acknowledgments   201

Selected Reading   203

Preface: A Man's Place Is in the Kitchen

Bringing that first baby home from the hospital, and settling into our new lives, Liz and I faced a nightly decision: one of us had to wrangle the newborn, and change the dirty diapers, and one of us had to make dinner. Like a lot of guys in my predicament—two-income family, wife working hard—I chose dinner and, without realizing it, new territory. My own father couldn't fry a burger, and Mom made nearly every home-cooked meal he ever ate, aligning my parents with 97.8 percent of the 185 human cultures studied by the first anthropologists to look into such matters, at least according to Richard Wrangham's *Catching Fire: How Cooking Made Us Human*. Wrangham admits that human males are perfectly capable of cooking, as evidenced by professional chefs and also by husbands helping out in "urban marriages." But he offers these exceptions to prove the rule, pointing out that even on tropical Vanatinai, a natural feminist paradise where both sexes hunted, fished, and fought wars, islanders still considered cooking "a low-prestige activity" meant for women alone, right down there with "cleaning up pig droppings." Wrangham places the source for this ancient division of labor—and marriage itself—deep in our evolutionary past, at about the time we discovered fire. The very project of cooking food, by this line of reasoning, called for a "primitive protection racket" whereby females did all the cooking and males rewarded them by making sure other men didn't steal the results.

For me to become the family cook, in other words—buy all the groceries, read all the cookbooks—meant taking on a role without a script. But it didn't feel optional. My father had worked long days at his law practice, so he'd never suffered even the slightest compunction to look busy in the evenings, and he'd never needed the domestic camouflage of the putatively productive but secretly calming chore. I had a wife working right alongside me, doing the same kind of journalism out of the same home office, but also doing the housecleaning and waking up five times a night to nurse the baby, and I had a conscience offering up the obvious thought-balloon: *Okay then, fuck it. Maybe I'll deal with my obvious inadequacy by taking full responsibility for seeing to it that our little family has a delicious, wholesome meal on the table, every single night, forever and ever, not least because Liz won't have the energy to make such a meal for at least a couple years.*

So far so good, but obsession, according to somebody who knew what he was talking about, binds anxiety. I had a long history of coping with change by going overboard on random new skills: forty-five thousand skateboard ollies had only barely gotten me through puberty; electric guitar, six hours a day, mostly Hendrix with a little Jimmy Page, barely soothed the psychic torture of being a pencil-necked, gap-toothed, freckle-faced redhead at a big California high school full of tan water-polo players. My father had been the same way: obsessive, not pencil-necked, studying bluegrass banjo in early middle age, to deal with his own domestic incarceration; rock climbing around the time I finished college, when his youth and strength threatened to fade. When I took on rock climbing myself, after graduation—summits appearing far more attainable than any actual life-goals—I got to feel both closer to my father and more in line with "an age that is obsessed with obsession," as Lennard J. Davis puts it. In *Obsession: A History*, Davis points out that we moderns tend to see obsession "both as a dreaded disease and as a noble and necessary endeavor"—precisely the way my father taught me to view my subsequent years in a surf town, burning my best energy on catching the right swell at the right combination of wind and tide.

But each new anxiety, in life, demands an appropriate diversion. So perhaps it was inevitable that, when I hit anxieties unfamiliar to my father, I would stumble onto equally alien obsessions. From the moment Liz and I blew all her savings on a tiny San Francisco fixer-upper, for example, it no longer mattered that I'd long considered three hours of surfing a daily minimum to keep me from completely losing my shit. I simply could not justify all that time at the beach. Cooking dinner, by contrast, even if I soiled every counter and pot and got plastered on some juicy new Zinfandel and pulled the old I-cooked-you-clean routine and then fell asleep on the couch, held out this gorgeous promise that a man might give back, prove his self-worth, even as he came to see preposterous wine and grocery bills as proud symptoms of his undying male vigor, fully expressed in the domestic sphere. He wouldn't even have to risk his neck on some mountain, or hide out at the corner pub, or slither down to the basement workshop, or go wherever guys had always gone when the baby wouldn't stop crying and he wasn't making enough money—like not *nearly* enough money—and he missed that serene bachelor pad and he wasn't sure he was really man enough to handle all this, even though he was, and he just didn't know it yet, and he loved his wife and his little girl, and he knew he'd die if he ever lost them or let them down. He could just cook and, through cooking, become a proper father and husband, an adult in the fullest sense.

That's a lot to ask of cooking, especially when time, money, and mess—cooking's primary costs—happen also to be the primary currencies of the contemporary marriage-with-newborn. It's one thing for Dad to grab Whole Foods takeout for everybody, in other words, or to whip together some quick, efficient little pasta while the wife bathes the baby, and then to grab that baby and read nighty-night books while the wife shoves all the dishes into the dishwasher and reads the *New Yorker* on the couch as you lie on the kid's floor desperately wishing the kid would, to quote the title of a recent bestseller, go the f—— to sleep. It's entirely another when he settles on cooking as a means to personal transformation, spending time, money, and mess, day after week after year, struggling to learn what the pro chefs know, not just because he wants to feed his family but because he won't be able to rest until he can whip out dinner-party meals of unassailably professional caliber, proving to himself and everyone else that, despite all the evidence, he really is still a man among men.

That's where this lack-of-a-road-map comes in: my father and I had always been close, and he'd long taken me for a masculine carbon copy of himself, always confident that a few key anecdotes, from his own life, would shine a light through my every dark tunnel. But when Dad realized that I'd back-burnered my climbing and surfing to master French sauce-reduction techniques, and pickling formulas, and the fat-to-lean ratios of Italian *salumi*, he sensed the first great gulf ever to grow between us. He began to look at me the way novelist Julian Barnes's father apparently looked at Barnes after the same discovery: with a "mild, liberal suspicion" that seemed to say, "If this is as bad as it gets . . . I can probably handle it." The key word, of course, being "probably," with its implication that one might *not* be able to handle it, so deeply does all this fancy-cooking bullshit suggest that one's son wasn't quite paying attention all those years, when you taught him how to be a man. I had been paying attention. But I was facing different circumstances and I was a different person. Unlike my father, I didn't just let my passions overtake my life; I let them *become* my life, at least until they'd run their unpredictable courses and then settled down, as cooking finally has, into a reasonably integrated part of my daily life.

PART ONE
The Burrito Years

1
You Are the Way You Eat

The aphorism most frequently repeated from Jean Anthelme Brillat-Savarin's 1825 warhorse, *The Physiology of Taste; or, Meditations on Transcendental Gastronomy*, has to be the one that goes, "Tell me what you eat and I shall tell you what you are." The old French glutton means something quite different, I believe, from today's more prudish (if linguistically more economical) "You are what you eat." The contemporary iteration expresses only a Puritanical Anglo-American view of food as fuel, or medicine, or poison, while Brillat-Savarin boasts rather of an insight he's had about the expression of cultural identity and aspiration through dining habits. It's the latter I find most useful in explaining my wife, at the time of our meeting. Exhibit A, first sighted on a knotty-pine bookshelf in the pretty young Elizabeth "Liz" Weil's own studio apartment, on a fine block in San Francisco's Mission District: *Joslyn Presents Bernard Schimmel's Masterpieces*, the obscure 1976 Continental cookery classic published by the Joslyn Art Museum of Omaha, Nebraska, where Liz's grandfather, Bernard Schimmel, had been the leading culinary light and bona-fide inventor of the Reuben sandwich, in honor of a poker buddy, Reuben Kulakofsky, a local Lithuanian-born grocer. (Brillat-Savarin, once again: "The discovery of a new dish does more for human happiness than the discovery of a star.") Liz told me this on our first date, after an indifferent dinner at a crepes joint and a follow-up drink at a fashionably sleazy dive bar. We were sitting nervously on Liz's perfectly respectable couch, talking fast like the earnest young bookworms we were, when she related a classic immigrant story. Bernard's father, Liz's own great-grandfather, had been raised in a hotel in Russia and come shuffling through Ellis Island before building four hotels along the midwestern rail lines: the Cornhusker, in Lincoln, Nebraska; the Hotel Lassen, in Wichita; the Blackstone, in Omaha; and the Hotel Custer, in Galesburg, Illinois. He'd then trained each son in a different hotel specialty—hospitality management, accounting—and he'd sent young Bernie to become the first American graduate from the famous hotel school in Lausanne, Switzerland, in 1928. When Bernie got back—tall and handsome, in Liz's framed black-and-white—a *cordon bleu* with an inordinate love for Scotch whisky, he'd married a Jewish girl named Beatrice and taken over the Custer, turning the Homestead Room into Illinois's leading Temple of Gastronomy. Live Maine lobsters on refrigerated rail cars, Blue Point oysters out of New York, fresh Italian truffles, in season: the Weils were understandably proud of this guy, and of the way he'd raised his three lovely daughters, Judy, Mary, and Connie, regionally midwestern and ethnically Jewish but gastronomically French, largely viewing the Reuben sandwich as nothing but a cute family sideshow.

Chain hotels and the rise of air travel, in Liz's telling of the family tale, crushed one Schimmel hotel after another. The last one standing was the Blackstone of Omaha, widely known as the finest hotel between Chicago and San Francisco, along the old Lincoln Highway. That's where all the Schimmels retreated, and that's where Bernie deigned to publish, for the benefit of Omaha's housewives, his tips for Sweetbreads à la Reine, Beignets au

Fromage, and Coquilles St. Jacques. Copies of *Schimmel* had since been given like a secular Torah to every one of Bernie's seven grandchildren, including Judy's youngest, the leggy, brown-haired young journalist passing all this along to me. Herself raised in Massachusetts, matured in Chicago, and devoted to marathon running and to clean, simple food, Liz had long since established a family Law of Nature by which Liz Hates Fancy French Cuisine So Don't Even Bother Trying To Make Her Eat It, and yet none of us can escape the way we've been raised: whether she liked it or not, she could order expertly in the finest of restaurants; her simplest plate of tomato-basil pasta revealed an artistic sensibility, and she certainly knew her *foie gras* from her *pistou*.

As for who I was, sitting on that couch and wishing I had the guts to make this beautiful girl stop talking and kiss me, there's more to learn from the "You are what you eat" formulation. I, too, had a great-grandfather come through Ellis Island, but as an illiterate Irish laborer bound for the New York slums. If you believe Jane Ziegelman's *97 Orchard: An Edible History of Five Immigrant Families in One New York Tenement*, that pretty much means he didn't have a food identity—as in, *none*, given that English oppression had long since replaced Irish cuisine with potatoes alone, and then, when those potatoes rotted in the wet Irish fields, with nothing at all ("How do you like the sound of *nothing* for dinner, you dirty fucking Irishman? Does *nothing* work for you *and* your ten dirty dying Irish children? Oh, excuse me, I have to go gorge on Beef Wellington"). Couple that with my father's comfortable upbringing in the Irish Catholic schools of 1950s Los Angeles, and with his mid-1980s bodybuilding obsession, when left-wing Berkeley lawyers were supposed to be out jogging or roller-skating, and you can see how divorced I was from any notion of food as joy, or ethnic identity. Dad would hit the gym after work, pump pyramid sets of bench press and bicep curls, building up those pecs and arms, and then he'd come home to chug a bottle of pre-digested protein and pick gingerly at Mom's cardboard pork chops (not her fault, just the way supermarket pork was, in the seventies). While I plowed everything Mom made, to convince her that she was a good cook and that we all loved her—true, on both accounts—Dad would leave the table, slip into the kitchen, and taper off with a jar of peanut butter, a jar of jelly, and a stick of butter, cycling through all three with the same spoon. Later, I would open the fridge, stare at Dad's plastic protein bottle, and ponder that word, "predigested," wondering why my own father drank vomit.

Thus, when a second date brought Liz over to my apartment, she found my refrigerator stocked as it always was with giant whole-wheat tortillas and recycled yogurt containers carrying precooked black beans, rice, salsa, and guacamole, so that I could whip out a vegetarian bean burrito for every day's lunch. As that second date led to a tenth, Liz discovered that I had exactly two dishes in my dinner rotation, each producing a single serving, un-less doubled: my Odd Nights Pasta, calling for three cups of dried penne, a single chopped tomato, half a diced red onion, two minced garlic cloves, and four sliced button mushrooms, typically followed by a bowl of cereal; and my Even Nights Stir Fry, calling for one cup of basmati rice, half a standard tofu brick, five broccoli florets, half a bell pepper, and a dollop of bottled Thai peanut sauce, also followed by a bowl of cereal. I could make some other stuff, like quesadillas and the occasional almond-butter-and-honey sandwich, and I was even proud of a little tofu-breading tech-nique I'd picked up from a vegan girlfriend, but all of this food pretty much sucked, and I'm not just playing for laughs when I say that I'd once made a date puke her guts out by mixing tofu and couscous with far too much cheap curry powder. I wish that were a joke, and that I were just a guy with a childish affinity for puke humor, but I'm telling it straight: tofu+couscous+too-much-curry=nauseated date. And hey, who knows, maybe she vomited for some other reason; maybe I made her nervous. That young lady was no Julia Child, either, specializing, as she did, in a Hungry Hippie breakfast of whole-wheat-and-canola-oil vegan pancakes with a side of soy bacon, a classic example of remorse cuisine—to steal a phrase from dear old Mollie Katzen, author of *The Moosewood Cookbook*, one of the half-dozen cookbooks I'd somehow accumulated by the time I met Liz, at which point my body was about 75 percent burrito by mass, the rest almost entirely consisting of Trader Joe's.

But here's the funny thing about who we are: it's never quite the same as who we want to be. Precisely because Liz came from that classy Jewish food family, she found my burritos thrilling, a way to break with a personal past she'd always found too fussy and ethnic (there'd been a fair amount of liver, too, in the Weil home). A lifetime of stir-fried tofu and cheap pasta sounded great, to her. And yet, precisely because I came from a family without a clear food identity, Liz's background offered a way for me to put on a little Ritz. Then there was the X-factor, ever present between two people forming a family: marriage creates a new micro-society with its own customs and rules, hashed out between the partners but influenced by unacknowledged sources, like our parents and the larger social classes we think we inhabit.

My mother, for example, cared mostly about how manifestly sane, kind, and lovely Liz appeared to be, and would've encouraged me to eat insects for the rest of my life, if that's what Liz's family wanted. "Look, sweetie, I don't want you to feel even the slightest pressure," Mom told me, after the very first time she met

Liz, "because I would never, ever want to meddle in your life, or be one of those terrible mothers who's always telling her son what to do, but I just want you to know that my mother left me quite a beautiful diamond wedding ring, and I've got it in the safety deposit box and I just want you to know that it's there for you, if you ever need it. You don't ever have to think it's a big deal or anything to ask me, and I won't make a fuss out of it if you do."

Me, weeks later: "Hey, Mom, how are you?"

"Fine, honey. What's up?"

"Nothing."

"Oh. Well, I'm glad you called."

"Yeah, how are you?"

"Everything's really good. Umm . . . let's see. I had a wonderful walk last night with your father, he was just so funny talking about . . ."

"I need the ring."

"Right."

"Today."

"Forty-five minutes, outside the Bank of America?"

"Bye."

I met my mother at the neighborhood branch across from Alice Waters's hallowed Chez Panisse. Mom handed me a blue velvet ring box like it was a meaningless brick we'd never discuss again.

Then she suggested lunch.

"Where?"

"Saul's?"

That would indeed be the only Jewish deli in the entire city of Berkeley.

"Matzo-ball soup?" she suggested, with a playful laugh.

To be fair, Saul's really was the obvious lunch spot in that neighborhood, and when Mom suggested a side of latkes, she openly cracked up, enjoying the tease. But the message was there, inside the joke: *Accommodate, my son. You'll never meet a better girl as long as you live, so eat whatever the hell these people like to eat, to make this lucky marriage soar.*

Then there was Liz's family, although I certainly didn't think of them while I was driving my crappy Toyota truck back over the Bay Bridge with a diamond in my pocket, all my energy focused on the proposal, and on getting to "Yes." I'd contemplated Grandma's rock long enough to figure it would suffice; I'd settled on the apartment building's roof for the proper place to pop the question; and I'd pictured Liz's pretty lips forming my desired answer. After that, however, I'd pictured nothing but joyous white light filling the scene, followed by years of undifferentiated bliss. Never once had I contemplated all the other human beings that a marriage proposal implicates, least of all the late Chef Schimmel's three daughters: Liz's mother, Judy, back in Wellesley, Massachusetts, screaming into the phone upon hearing the news; Liz's Aunt Connie, across the bay in Piedmont, likewise screaming into the phone; and Liz's Aunt Mary, living near their mom, Bea, in Omaha, where the Blackstone had long since been sold to the Radisson chain and, finally, turned into an office building. Aunt Mary not only screamed, she asked the pressing question on every Schimmel girl's mind: filet mignon, rack of lamb, or salmon, at the reception?

The Weils, in other words, did not exactly take Liz out for tacos to celebrate her union to this California surfer. Judy had boots on the ground in San Francisco within two weeks, knocking out the flower contract *and* the wedding dress before lunch on the first morning. Liz's father, Doug, a dedicated gourmand, golfer, and real estate investor—who had perhaps loved his father-in-law's cooking more than anybody—then drove us all around the greater Bay Area to look at the grassy outdoor wedding spots Liz and I liked. Judy, meanwhile, strategized about how to cope with Grandma Bea's inevitable objections—not to my being a gentile, but to the far more serious family-cultural breach of Liz's wanting an outdoor wedding in the middle of the day, instead of a black-tie affair in a grand hotel.

"And the coffee," Judy asked the dazed manager of a casual coastal California inn, at two o'clock that very afternoon, "how will you serve the coffee?"

"Well, ma'am, typically, we do a very nice coffee buffet with hot-pot thermoses and cups and saucers and cream in silver creamers, but . . . I suppose we could have table service, if . . ."

"Table service."

"And Dan," asked Judy, on our return drive toward the Golden Gate and San Francisco, as the autumn darkness settled over the commute-hour freeway. "Have you thought about how you're going to raise the kids, in terms of religion?"

Traffic so clogged the road, and the air in the car had become so thick, that Doug had an inspiration: Why not pull into that there mall and start in on the wedding registry?

I should say up front, before I describe the scene, that I'd never really eaten sugar-glazed jumbo pretzels. In fact, I'd never heard of sugar-glazed jumbo pretzels. But something about standing in that crowded Crate & Barrel, anxiety mounting as I gazed across pile upon pile of purple, pink, and yellow plates and white and blue bowls and green mugs, violet soup tureens and shining steel knife holders and leather-clad ice buckets and white plastic spice racks and calico kitchen towels and cheap Martini glasses and dish-drying racks and stainless-steel blenders, gave me a desperate jones for a snack, a really big snack.

"You don't have to get involved in this," Doug said to me, in his first of many kindnesses. "Just let the girls have fun."

Excusing myself, I stepped into the flow of shoppers in that mall's pedestrian walkway, marching fast until I saw the local Wetzel's Pretzels franchise. Moments later, I returned to Crate & Barrel, with liquid sugar glinting white on my chin, and asked Doug if he'd like a bite—"'s really amazingly good, I mean, you just wouldn't believe how good, you sure? You sure you don't want a bite? I mean, okay, okay, but don't be shy, because, in fact, I think maybe I'll just pop on back and score another one of these babies and, man, I'd be so happy to score a honey-glazed for you, too, Doug. Or even Judy—any interest? Sugar-glazed? I mean, I'm sure they've got other kinds . . ."

Nothing came of that night, no list of goodies, thanks largely to Liz's understanding that my sugar-glazed pretzel mania had to be a cry for help. But we found our way to Williams-Sonoma weeks later, for the confusing experience of picking out an entire kitchen's worth of great gear with the reasonable expectation that the lion's share might magically appear from UPS. I'd never before bought anybody a wedding present. Berkeley weddings tended toward a polite request for donations to an elementary school in the Guatemalan Highlands, and at the few normal weddings I'd attended, I'd always been too cheap even to ask how the registry process worked. So I discovered only at Williams-Sonoma the food-centric nature of the middle-class American wedding registry at the dawn of the twenty-first century. The primary purpose of marriage, it appeared, was not child rearing so much as home entertaining dependent upon professional-grade culinary equipment affordable only by an entire community's pitching in. At Williams-Sonoma, where avaricious couples just like ourselves (or, rather, like me, as Liz didn't find kitchen gear all that interesting)

bumped elbows in the aisles trying to pretend this perverse combination of conspicuous consumption and lottery-style windfall
was simply a very serious matter of good middle-class values, I
discovered that cooking equipment marked status in a language
known to every couple who'd registered in the prior ten years.
Every upscale kitchenware chain offered precisely the same five
strata of every kind of gear, most obviously in the pan depart-
ment. So as we browsed the aisles, and noticed some super-skinny
good-looking couple in expensive shoes checking off the Copper
Core 11-inch Sauteuse, we knew without a doubt not only that
they were richer than ourselves, but that they also had richer
friends and family, because we were only looking at the 5-Ply
Stainless collection. Knives were a bit of an exception—nobody
wanted to gift the murder weapon, and the pricey Japanese up-
grades hadn't yet hit those stores—but it was absolutely true of
appliances, where we had to gauge the gamble of listing that four-
hundred-dollar toaster. Nothing ventured, nothing gained, of
course, and Liz might well have had an aunt or uncle willing to go
big, but we also risked offending all seventy-five of the people that
I personally had invited to the wedding, as they all asked each
other the reasonable question such a listing would raise. To wit:
Who the fuck does that asshole think we are?

Liz and I lived together during that year of engagement, but
we had a lot on our minds besides food: the mounting financial
disaster of that eviction lawsuit, for example, as our home's then-
current tenants, a pair of graduate students, decided they were in
fact the victimized proletariat under capitalist assault from yuppie
scum, and therefore had a moral obligation to all mankind to make
sure that Dan and Liz either paid an enormous cash settlement to
make them move or else found the experience of moving into
their own very first home, to start a family, so morbidly painful

and costly that nobody else would ever consider it, and real estate would return to its rightful owners, the People. Once that was all over, our energy went into blowing the remainder of Liz's money on a carpenter's doing what I could not yet do myself: lace up the work boots, strap on the old tool belt, crank some tunes, suck a few bong hits, and fix up yet another home, for yet another pretty young woman. We had to eat, of course, but we mostly patronized cheap ethnic joints in perfect conformity with our young/liberal/creative peer group: Indian food one night, Thai the next. Once a week or so, we snuck beers and relatively quiet handheld foods (burritos, falafel, nothing with a loud wrapper) into art-house movie theaters.

This lack of culinary focus created a vacuum easily filled by Judy and Doug, who flew out once a month to work on wedding plans and treat us to grand Francophile meals at great San Francisco restaurants like Gary Danko, Charles Nob Hill, Zuni Café, and Boulevard. I had a doctor tell me, at about this time, that I'd officially become an Overweight American with High Cholesterol, and that does dampen one's gastronomic enthusiasm. Plus, every time I'd gone to a decent restaurant with my own family, growing up, there'd always been stern looks and cleared throats to make sure that nobody ever got the foolish idea it would be okay to order a starter, and that everybody noticed the bargain-priced burger at the bottom of the entrée list, a perfectly fine choice for the entire family. Worse still were the nights when my grandparents took us to the Burlingame Country Club, where even kids had to wear a tie. My hippie parents, despite knowing this, never once made me arrive with a tie, so I always had to wear some heinous blood-red knit tie kept by the maître d' as a kind of Scarlet Letter, announcing to all the members eating their curiously shitty food in the club's dining room that I Do Not

Belong. That's where my sister Kelly, a born Child of Nature, once leaned over to sniff her ridiculous shrimp cocktail. Grandma flinched in horror and then whacked Kelly in the back of her pretty head, smashing Kelly's freckled nose into that canned cocktail sauce. Kelly looked up in astonishment, smeared with blood-red goop. Dad marched out of the club to avoid punching somebody. Mom bent over and sniffed the hell out of her Cobb Salad, in protest. And I developed a deep-seated association between fancy dining rooms and rage, and a total inability to link formality with pleasure.

Liz's own anti-*Schimmel* ordering habits reinforced this killjoy attitude—calibrated, as were hers, toward hammering home the point that she could not be corralled into putting silly undue emphasis on expensively stuffing her face, nor could she be talked into having even one itty-bitty little teeny-tiny taste of a single, solitary dish that didn't interest her. But after a few fine-dining restaurants in which I copied my betrothed, hoping to fit in, Liz explained that I was going about it all wrong. The proper way to show gratitude to her parents was to order exactly what I felt like eating, price be damned. I didn't have a clue what I felt like eating because I didn't even recognize most of the words on the menus. I also sensed that restaurant ordering, in the company of Doug, Judy, and old Bernie's ghost, served as a proving ground, an arena for the demonstration of culinary insight and, just as readily, culinary stupidity. If you picked well, murmuring approval might burble forth; if your dish sucked, and you admitted as much, you would learn that Doug and Judy and even Liz had all had doubts about the Baked Pasta with Nettles and Duck Confit from the moment they'd looked at the menu. So, with Doug's big-hearted encouragement—*Order like a man, my boy! Ignore these waist-watching ladies and party with me!*—I began copying my new mentor-and-benefactor's every move, swinging for the fences with the seared foie gras and fig appetizer, the Kobe filet mignon with sauce Bordelaise and shaved black truffle, the peach crème brûlée. And that's how old Bernie's legacy—and Doug's generosity—awakened me for the first time to the fact that a human mouth can deliver astonishing pleasure. And yet, fawning enthusiasm was not the Weil way. In order to fit in, I had to sit there all calm and collected, pretending that I could make a discriminating comparison of this particular *foie gras torchon* against every other I'd ever eaten, and maybe even the foie served by Judy's own father at Judy's own fancy-hotel wedding, when all I really wanted to do was scream and writhe like a Pentecostal tongue-talker, praising the Lord with choking sobs of ecstatic gratitude for keeping me alive long enough to experience mouthfuls of enlarged goose liver washed down by Château d'Yquem Sauternes.

Doug phoned, eventually, from the wedding caterer's office. He and Judy were up in Sonoma tasting menu possibilities without us because I was maintaining the ruse, for the sake of my bride-to-be, that I still shared her disinterest in pigging out on fine free food at every opportunity.

As it happened, Doug had a question about cake.

"I really don't care," Liz said into the phone. "I have absolutely no opinion." Then she turned to me and said, "You don't either, right, honey? What kind of cake we have?"

"Ah . . ."

"I mean, I'd just as soon not even have a cake."

"What do you mean?"

"I never even like wedding cakes. They're never any good. I might rather have a cobbler."

"A wedding cobbler?"

"What's wrong with that?"

"Tell your dad I like lemon cake."

She looked at me funny. "You're serious?"

"Tell him."

"You really want me to tell my father that."

"I do."

She did. Then Liz rubbed her eyes, looked away from me, and said, to the wall but really to me, "Okay, so now my dad wants to know how lemony."

"Super fucking lemony."

"He's putting the baker on the phone."

Liz handed me the handset, and I discovered, to my own surprise, that I absolutely did not want this baker putting artificial flavoring into the white cake itself, but that I'd love to have the buttercream frosting and buttercream filling carry a knockout lemony punch.

Then came the Big Day, which really was the happiest day of my life, up until that point—the very first thing I'd ever done that felt positively, unequivocally like the Right Move. My folks threw a terrific West Coast barbecue the night before, with live country music and one of Dad's new climbing buddies dressed up in a bear costume, hoping to rattle all the visiting East Coasters. The next morning, the sun shone down on the green lawns at the appointed hour. Liz's regal Grandma Beatrice flinched at my surf buddies in their "dress-up" silk Hawaiian shirts and their best flip-flops. My grandfather toasted not the bride and groom, nor even the bride's family, but his very own law firm. And the very first thing I did, at the ceremony's glorious end, was to beat all the guests in a mad sprint to the raw oyster bar. Nobody had yet told me that a touch of class called for letting others go first—that hospitality toward friends and family was the whole point—so I plowed about a dozen Point Reyes oysters before I let anybody else get near the half-shells. Then, seeing the line patiently building behind me, I felt the very same shame—the identical awareness of a misstep—as that described by Francine Prose in *Gluttony*. Recounting how she and her husband joined a friend in eating three plates of oysters at a large cocktail party, Prose says that she overheard another guest say, "They've eaten *all* the oysters." Mortified by the error, she and her husband fled the party "as hurried and guilty as Adam and Eve fleeing Eden in a Renaissance painting."

As A. J. Liebling has pointed out, in describing the challenges of the non-professional eater trying to consume professional portions, oysters offer "no problem, since they present no bulk." For this reason, I had plenty of room to make myself the only wedding guest demanding not just a second but a third helping of the rack of lamb with more and more Pinot Noir, all provided by Doug and Judy.

I was cutting into the gorgeous yellow wedding cake, congratulating myself on my choice of in-laws, when I saw a sterling opportunity for a display of the selfless mensch-like concern for others that was going to make me such a terrific addition to their family: handing that second slice (after the one for my wife) to my new father-in-law.

"Oh, no thanks," Doug said. "I actually hate lemon."

"Sweetheart," I hissed quietly to Liz, "why on earth did you allow me to insist on a lemon cake, knowing your father hates lemon?"

She had a great answer: Old Bernie, it turned out, loved lemon so much he always kept lemon drops in his pocket, even had lemon boughs on his coffin. "My mom loves lemon, too," Liz told me. "It's her favorite thing. So you got huge points."

2
On the Cookbook as Scripture

Most of us own cookbooks we never use, largely because we buy cookbooks for reasons other than a clear intent to cook from them—as mementos, maybe, from some beloved restaurant, or in aspiration toward a given lifestyle. I'd acquired Mollie Katzen's all-vegetarian *Moosewood Cookbook*, for example, despite being neither vegetarian nor a cook, because the Moosewood Restaurant happened to be the best restaurant in my college town of Ithaca, New York, where Katzen taught generation after generation of bright young things to think of her Russian Cabbage Borscht as a thrilling cultural experience. As for the two slab-like amber volumes of *The Gourmet Cookbook*, compiled by the magazine's editors from recipes published in their pages, they caused me a sick self-hatred because, every time I saw them, I remembered the day my grandfather and his second wife moved to an old-folks home. I'd been mostly focused on grabbing everything of value he'd meant to leave for the Goodwill, including those miserable books. Even my three Alice Waters cookbooks had come into my life for goofy reasons: she'd been my Montessori preschool teacher, in Berkeley, before she opened my hometown's most famous restaurant, Chez Panisse. I'd felt a certain pride in that—like somebody who's once been a schoolmate of a president, and who therefore buys that president's biography because its presence on a shelf will generate warm feelings of connectedness to power.

Most of the time, when a cookbook finally does draw you into the recipes, the reasons remain mysterious; but sometimes we can easily identify why a given text electrifies us, at a given time in our lives. Take *Chez Panisse Vegetables*, an austere, vaguely totalitarian, shiny-black hardback arranged A–Z, from Amaranth Greens (Wilted) to Zucchini (Pasta, with Walnuts and Pesto). I'd carried *Chez Panisse Vegetables* from apartment to apartment, throughout my twenties, without any inkling that it would someday be the portal through which Alice began to whisper into my ear. I'd carried it along in our U-Haul, too, when Liz and I finally parked in front of our asbestos-clad, peak-roofed, child's drawing of a two-flat house. Tenants still occupied the downstairs flat, so we schlepped everything up the front steps into our sunny, four-room, 750-square-foot apartment. The front door opened into a short central hallway with a cozy bedroom on each side. At the hallway's end, on the right, another small door led into a small living room, while the left-hand wall opened into a cheerful kitchen where *Chez Panisse Vegetables* spent months on a shelf, performing a duty akin to that expected of any other knickknack.

When I did open *Vegetables*, I sought help only with my Odd Nights Pasta, the one with the tomato. I'd noticed that whenever Liz made tomato pasta, it was terrific. My old stand-by paled. So I'd flipped open *Vegetables*, turned toward *T*, for tomato, and, because the moment had not yet come, felt not the faintest temptation toward Champagne Tomato Salad, Tomato and Basil Bruschetta, Tomato and Cantal Cheese Galette, Italian Tomato and Bread Soup, nor even Chilled Tomato Soup. I just followed Alice's instructions for Garden Tomato and Garlic Pasta, dicing three "perfectly ripe tomatoes," peeling and chopping three cloves of garlic and a bunch of basil leaves, and then accepting Alice's entirely novel command to "have all the ingredients prepared and ready by the stove." Next up, I set a "heavy-bottomed skillet" on a burner, lit the burner with a match, and glugged in a *half cup* of extra-virgin olive oil, which completely blew my mind. That was basically all that was left in our bottle, and it was probably like a full dollar's worth and about four hundred calories: *Man, okay,* I thought, *this is some serious restaurant-style cooking.* But I did as told: warming the oil first, tossing in the garlic and "right away, before the garlic starts to brown," adding the tomatoes and stirring, which completely confused me, because I'd always, always browned garlic. I'd thought that was the whole point. Equally perplexing: Alice said the tomatoes "will probably spatter a little," and they didn't. Oil not hot enough, apparently. But, onward: add the basil and "cook just a minute or two, until the tomatoes are warmed through and have started to relax."

Tomatoes, relaxing?

"Hey, will you remind me," Liz said, as we ate with the back door open to the warm dusk, "why we want to wait a few more years to have a baby?"

A first hint, in other words, of the anxiety that would soon make *Vegetables*—and, therefore, tomato relaxation—a worthy place to hide. Overall, however, we were leading what I considered the idyllic life: Liz wrote magazine articles in one of the front bedrooms while I flailed at writing the Great American Novel in the other. We used our little living room as a bedroom, and our life felt like an unbroken stream of interesting work, movies, exercise, romantic bliss, and beer. Liz didn't much care for wine, but she loved a good IPA, especially after a long run in

Golden Gate Park. So I couldn't fathom why anybody would pursue change, much less the headache of cooking actual recipes. But then it began:

"Just remind me," Liz said. "I'm getting confused. When we said a couple years, did we mean a couple years to birth or conception?"

"More pasta?"

"I don't want to be an old parent."

"I'll get you pasta."

"But tell me how long you really want to wait, just so I know."

"I love our life the way it is."

"Two years?"

Shortly thereafter, for the first time in my whole entire chickenshit existence, I was a young man with a happily pregnant wife. Two weeks later still, giddy with hope and excitement, Liz drove herself clear across San Francisco to the Kaiser Permanente hospital for the initial prenatal checkup—letting me take a pass because she's great like that, always joking that she ought to be more of a demanding, high-maintenance bitch, but constitutionally incapable of being anything but accommodating. Meanwhile, I sat at my desk—a solid-core door supported by two cheap file cabinets—looking out my tall window at the yellow house on the other side and trying not to hyperventilate, thinking I was totally screwed and I had to finish this novel *so fast* before my life ended and I had to get a lobotomy and become a CPA just to pay the bills and then slip into a depression and kill myself because I'm not capable of adapting to any existence except the absolutely perfectly orderly and peaceful one I'd already gotten mastered before I somehow lost my way and agreed to have a baby.

The phone rang: Liz, sobbing, saying the sonogram found only what they'd called a "blighted ovum." No heartbeat, in other words. No baby.

I wasn't a total pig, so I felt a freaky admixture of intense concern for my hurting girl, average-to-middling sorrow about our lost pregnancy, and weirdly exuberant relief, as if I'd gotten a death sentence commuted by God. But then I saw Liz walking down the crummy sidewalk all dressed in white, with her black hair shining and her eyes all red as she hugged herself and cried openly and hurried up our shitty, rotting steps to rush in the front door before the neighbors saw. She went straight into the living room, threw herself onto our bed, wept some more, and told me she felt certain she'd never bear children, and that her teenaged anorexia had somehow ruined everything. She now wanted nothing more in the universe than to be a mother and couldn't possibly wait another second without losing her mind.

Two months later, and now a serious crackerjack with that tomato technique, I managed to feign excitement when Liz got pregnant yet again, though less so over the surprising new emotional imperative she felt toward yet another elective responsibility of the kind I'd always eschewed: Liz needed a puppy, she told me, right away, so that she'd have something to love throughout this pregnancy, regardless of what happened to the baby.

"Now wait," I said, "hold on, this is an emotional time, but is that really a great idea? Because, I mean, I'm going to flip the first time I have to skip surfing to walk a dog."

Liz dropped eight hundred bucks—far more than I could've gotten for my pickup—on an English setter puppy, a dog so comically cute it looked like a Disney creation, all black-and-white and silky smooth, with long soft hair and floppy ears and big floppy feet. She named the dog Sylvie, and as Liz's belly began to swell, we walked Sylvie together in the park atop Bernal Hill. It happened to be late winter just then, a time of year resembling spring in other parts of North America: grass greening up from the rains, a few poppies and other wildflowers appearing tiny on the steep slopes, and little white butterflies driving our bird-dog puppy crazy. Liz and I would stop on our walks to chat about which showing of which new-release movie we ought to catch that night. Then we'd gaze out over San Francisco's sweeping-flat Mission District. Off to the left, pastel homes swept up the green hillsides of Twin Peaks, where my mother had grown up. Dead ahead, due north, we could see the downtown office towers where my grandfather had been a lawyer. We could see the gun-metal gray of the Bay Bridge, too, arcing eastward into Berkeley. But mostly that view was about airy impermanence, for me, all the old wooden houses, rising and falling on the undulating San Francisco landscape like windblown sea foam on the swells, lifting into a sky equally changeable, by the day and the hour, with the constant coming and going of the white fog banks, blowing past our hill in bits and pieces.

Socializing tends to fall off as the pregnant lady grows increasingly fatigued. Falafel and burritos become unattractive to the pregnant lady's palate. Pancakes migrate from the breakfast menu to lunch and even dinner. Movie rentals displace theatergoing, for the increased comfort of the pregnant lady's own couch, and also for the greater access to ice cream. But even here, a book like *Vegetables* can't quite get a man's attention, given that nostalgia for his lost life-about-town pushes non-pancake food conversation in the direction of, say, "Sweetheart? If I could ever figure out how to make a vegetarian kung pao like we used to order at Eric's on Church back when we ever, ever went out to dinner, do you think you'd be interested?"

Nora Ephron, screenwriter of the classic romantic comedy *When Harry Met Sally* and of the movie adaption of *Julie & Julia*, Julie Powell's memoir of cooking every recipe in Julia Child's *Mastering the Art of French Cooking*, has admitted that, after she got married, she "entered into a series of absolutely pathological culinary episodes. I wrapped things in phyllo. I stuffed grape leaves. There were soufflés. I took a course in how to use a Cuisinart food processor." My own such episodes began with a search in that dark-and-dirty basement, underneath our tenants' flat, among all my old climbing gear, and my neglected surfboards, in order to find Liz's old wok. Then came a cursory glance at *A Spoonful of Ginger*, by Nina Simonds, and a whole new tofu technique: pressing it in paper towels under a weight, to leach out excess water; then slicing and frying it hot, so it wouldn't stick to the wok and disintegrate like it had all throughout my graduate school years; broccoli boiled a little first, and then tossed in tender, and then, *boom*, a bellyful.

Still, the drumbeat deepens, the Anxiety Army grows closer. Natural nesting instincts provoked Liz to wish we had at least a few flower boxes beautifying the little patch of concrete we called a front yard. I wasn't about to get punked by an actual carpenter again, so I bought *Better Homes and Gardens Step-by-Step Basic Carpentry* along with a Skil "worm-drive" circular saw, a "contractor grade" hammer, a "contractor grade" tape measure, and an embarrassingly new tool belt. I built and then hated and then destroyed and then rebuilt my first flower box about five times, anxious to get it right. Liking the outlet, I tackled our three-story back-stair assembly, a rickety pile running from our top-level flat down past the tenants' street-level unit and then on down to the basement/backyard level: rotten to the core, it turned out, far too dangerous for my pregnant girl. Endless rookie-carpenter screwups meant endless lumberyard trips—and an alarming number of carcinogenic asbestos-siding tiles breaking off the back of the house, releasing their toxic particles into the air. But an underemployed man in that position craves the excuse to put his head down and work like hell with his own body and hands, while his baby grows closer and a few thousand more of the wife's dollars get spent on still more cool tools during early-morning drives out to the manly world of a place like Sierra Point Lumber, where I could smell the salty-cool bay and see the bright white fog up on San Bruno Mountain and learn how to speak confidently of two-by-eights and framing angles.

Liz really was a nauseous pregnant lady, and she didn't always want vegetarian kung pao, so I did make that Garden Tomato and Garlic Pasta once in a while. I came to appreciate the quick and definitive way in which Alice had made me markedly better at a useful and tolerably masculine chore that also included filling up my belly. But still, the conditions weren't yet right for total *Vegetables* immersion. Even if I did think of building on my positive tomato experience, I didn't consider doing it through Alice's Beet-Green Pasta, or Broccoli Raab Pasta. I had not the slightest idea what beet greens and broccoli raab even were, but they both sounded healthy, and therefore I could not see how either could be worth eating—an adult version of the three-year-old's view, *Even though Mommy wants me to taste bacon, I've never heard of it, so it's probably rat poison.* So I tried to replicate that Garden Tomato competence-experience in ways that called for no meaningful change in my self: seeking out a book to help me tackle this other go-to restaurant dish we'd both liked in our pre-pregnancy days, the Chicken Tikka from Shalimar. *The Bombay Cafe*, by Neela Paniz, led us to the discovery of an old dusty Indian grocery in the Mission District, bringing self-congratulation at being so urban-adventurous, and then repeated mention of same to our friends ("And you've just *got* to check out this amazing old Indian shop on Valencia"). Paniz had included a few other Indian-restaurant standards—Lentil Dahl, Curried Eggplant—so Liz suspended her pancake preference just long enough for me to acquire a complete Indian spice collection, including pounds of whole cardamom pods green and black.

Then we turned a critical corner. While we were lying in bed one night, in our living room, Liz put my palm over the lovely bare skin of her belly.

Boom! I felt a kick so firm that it pulsed through my skin up my arm into my brain as a crystal-clear message from my daughter-to-be, saying, "Wake up, asshole! It's time to give up on the novel and sell that beater truck and get a real job!"

Late in the seventh month, as I tracked a pot of basmati rice with my digital-watch timer and screwed down the very last of the back-stair handrails with a power drill, my father asked if I felt ready for fatherhood.

I said, "Nope, but I don't have to be. I have five more weeks. I'm maturing right on schedule, and I'll be ready when the baby comes."

Dad asked, "If the baby comes early?"

"I'll never mature. I'll remain forever stuck, five weeks short of full emotional adulthood."

The very next day, still not seeing how a cookbook might provide all the medicine I needed, I woke up, had breakfast, and demolished the front stairs in about an hour—crowbar, wrecking bar, Skilsaw, ripping that structure right to the ground. This meant Liz had to climb down a ladder to her next ob-gyn checkup, but I thought I was golden for at least a month. Then my cell phone rang. It was Liz, telling me that our baby wasn't fattening fast enough. The brains and the bones were on track, but the kid was just too skinny. By the time I showed up at the hospital, scared witless, doctors had found symptoms of preeclampsia, a mysterious syndrome often fatal to the baby, sometimes fatal to the mother, and incurable without immediate delivery. They shot up Liz with labor-inducing medication and told me it might take twelve hours for the contractions to begin.

A few hours later, when nothing had happened, Liz encouraged me to take a break. So I left the hospital and devoured a *carne asada* super-burrito and walked the puppy on grassy Bernal Hill, up the block from our house. I felt out-of-body anxious in the heat of a San Francisco Indian summer. Then I walked home and, as if it made any sense at all, buckled on my tool belt.

Liz called and said, "I just have a feeling stuff's going to start happening."

Once his baby's born, and brought home, a young father discovers that his daily life now offers a lot of time for reflective thought. Not that you're capable of having any thoughts—too little sleep—but hour upon hour passes with nobody really interested in the content of your mind. Sort of amazing: you go from perfect intimacy, claiming that girl's attention for yourself, to zero intimacy, as the baby's claim takes over. Weirder still, the breast-feeding wife looks terrific, thinning down under the immense caloric demands of nursing even as her breasts grow to record sizes, and yet it does her man no good whatsoever. Throw in a dog and it's not long before it occurs to you that your own needs fall well below even those of the canine, in the family's prioritization scheme. In fact, you are the sole member of the household with zero needs scheduled to be met by any other member of the household. And that's the context in which I began flipping cookbook pages uneasily: first in *The Bombay Kitchen* and *A Spoonful of*

Ginger, pondering the idea that I might somehow become a truly accomplished cook of either Indian or Chinese cuisine, during the dark passage ahead. *Rick Bayless's Mexican Kitchen* presented a similar new identity—Guacamole King—but when taken together these options felt too painfully similar to the cultural anomie that had driven my fellow Californian, John Walker Lindh, growing up across the Golden Gate Bridge in Marin County, to become the American Taliban: *Wow, gee, I mean, I guess I could be a Buddhist if I wanted—shave my head, wear pink robes, all that cool Zen shit—or wait! I know! I'll go Muslim! That'll show my dumb-ass hippie parents!*

I'd done my share of yoga, in other words, but not nearly enough to justify still more simmering of onions and tomatoes, nor the endless employment of the same dried-up and dusty spices shipped across the planet to make the only kind of Indian cuisine I knew. Ditto for Chinese. I liked that kung pao just fine, but national cuisines occupy value niches somewhere down in our lizard brains; they have emotional meaning, such that an upper-middle-class white kid's fervent allegiance for, say, Ethiopian food, cannot be interpreted as a mere fondness for flatbread. I probably could've dabbled in Spanish cuisine, see, because that would've satisfied my trained preference for all things European; Italian would've been better; German, not so much; Hungarian, *fuck that.*

Chez Panisse Vegetables, on the other hand . . . I turned it over in my lap and looked at the author photo. Alice, the woman Anthony Bourdain once described as "Pol Pot in a muumuu," seemed deeply familiar, like an old family friend I hadn't seen in ages. The twinkle in the eyes, the sharp and smart smile—very much like my mother's. If I squinted just right, I could tell myself this wasn't simply a random choice or the obvious bestseller. I was returning to my roots, cooking the classic food of my childhood village. Flipping to the table of contents, I began to wonder why I'd always cooked so few recipes from any one of my cookbooks. I had some kind of filter, clearly, through which I scanned a cookbook's recipes, rejecting all but one or two until something grabbed my eye. But I'd never asked myself to justify the criteria for this filtering. All I knew is that it went something like this: Roasted Winter Vegetables, from *Chez Panisse Vegetables*? No way. I couldn't name a single winter vegetable; therefore they all had to be gross. Cabbage and Bean Soup with Duck Confit? Vaguely recall eating confit with Doug and Judy, but no clue what the word "confit" even means, and therefore no interest in learning. So why not eliminate the filter of me and accept, in its place, the filter of Alice? Why not, in other words, accept that if the great Alice Waters figured a recipe belonged in her cookbook, it was definitely worth making at least once? Ephron writes of a certain Holy Trinity of cookbooks in her life: Julia Child's *Mastering the Art of French Cooking*; Craig Claiborne's *The New York Times Cookbook*, and Michael Field's *Cooking School*. Alice has since told me that she took the same approach with books from Elizabeth David, Richard Olney, Madeleine Kamman, Lulu Peyraud, and Roy Andries de Groot. It always had to be French, with People Like Us: ancient Revolutionary sympathies, maybe, between our two countries; shared antipathy toward the English. Funny, though, when I thought about it: not a single major French population center in the United States; France the only European nation never to have sent us a big immigrant wave; and yet French language so widely (and mysteriously) taught in our schools. Just the right non-participant status, perhaps, in the great elbow-jostling of Ellis Island; just the right positioning as every American's cultural ancestors but nobody's personal ancestors. Eat dinner at some Brooklyn Italian restaurant a hundred years ago, or drink Guinness in some midcentury

Boston Irish pub, and you entered an immigrant's world. Spend big on French food, and not so much. Fancy, foreign, exotic, but not too exotic. Take the Beck family in Samuel Chamberlain's classic *Clementine in the Kitchen*, the 1943 novel of an American diplomatic family, after years in France, forced back to Boston by the war. Clementine, their beloved French chef, comes along, bringing "everything from a rare edition of Brillat-Savarin" to her "gleaming copper *batterie de cuisine*," earthen casseroles, and knives. Stateside, Clementine laments the absent French ingredients but marvels at the New England seafood; soon, the Beck family throws a dinner party and Clementine's food so dazzles that it propels the Becks into the higher social orders of their town.

In any case, I began to wonder if *Vegetables* might play such a role in my own life—not social catapult so much as the job performed by Ephron's Holy Trinity and Alice's Jackson Five, that of the personal culinary scripture. Objectively speaking, there's something a little heartless about *Vegetables*. The recipes work beautifully, they embody a remarkably complete and timeless approach to plant foods, and yet they seem studiously to avoid any evidence of having emerged from a particular mind at a particular time. If you were in a cynical frame of mind, the natural conclusion might be that somebody simply canvassed recipes from all the Chez Panisse cooks and wrote up an introduction. If you weren't, you might deduce that this was an intentional way of positioning the book as a classic. And I was definitely not in a cynical frame of mind; I was in the same state of spiritual yearning that got Lindh flying to Pakistan and learning to fieldstrip an AK-47, in hopes of slaughtering the Infidel. The very impersonality of *Vegetables*, in other words, allowed me to read it as *supra*-personal, as if it were not just a marquee title by America's most influential cook but rather my own hometown's time-tested manual for domestic excellence. Viewed in that light, the book's A–Z quality—inviting me to cook every recipe therein—felt like a gift, presenting a crystal-clear path to a body of knowledge that appeared just as complete and compelling as *Mein Kampf* has to other vulnerable souls, at other vulnerable moments.

PART TWO
The Alice Years

3
Recipes Are for Idiots Like Me

Anybody who's ever loved a cookbook—*truly* loved a cookbook, every page a wonderland—has met one of those depressing Recipes Give Me a Headache people, like a particular friend of my father's. A Berkeley lawyer I'll call Lisa, she happened to count Alice among her sometimes clients. So I mentioned to Lisa this plan of mine, with *Vegetables*. I told her that Liz had been slipping ever deeper into sleepless confusion, and no longer cared much what I made for dinner, as long as I cooked a lot of it quickly and kept ample ice cream around. As a result, I'd begun to find my legs in the kitchen, savoring especially my newfound authority to make a mess while I ripped through such oddities as Brussels Sprouts Pasta, Chanterelle Pasta, or something called Chard, Spinach, and Escarole Pasta.

"And when you cook," asked Lisa, "how closely do you follow Alice's recipes?"

"Spot-on religiously," I replied.

Take Wild Mushroom Pasta Gratin, a kitchen-destroying combination of mushrooms, cream, and noodles, which I'd slammed out right after Whole-Wheat Pasta with Cauliflower, Walnuts, and Ricotta Salata, and right before the ultimately tragic Wild Mushroom and Greens Ravioli (more soiled pots and cluttered counters than you'd believe; amateurs shouldn't fuck around with ravioli). I'd started by pushing aside some dirty lunch dishes to make room for a bowl filled with hot water and precisely one ounce of dried porcinis, which turned out to be three expensive bags' worth, because each bag hardly weighed anything. Liz was bathing little Hannah in a tiny plastic tub while I opened the fridge and rummaged around for butter. Then I portioned out precisely one tablespoon of butter and located our smallest saucepan—likewise in the sink—and scrubbed it clean. While the butter melted, I dug around in the sink yet again, fishing out measuring spoons still dirty from buttermilk pancakes. I found the flour where I'd left it during the very same project, and I measured one tablespoon of that flour into the butter. Liz was nursing Hannah while I measured out a shocking *cup* of heavy cream—cardiovascular suicide, as far as I could tell. Then there was this unusual move of spooning in two to three tablespoons of that porcini rehydration water— mushroomy flavor, I guessed—and clearing still more crap off the stove to free up yet another burner for simmering the cream, porcini water, flour, and butter, together with a little store-bought chicken stock. While it was all bubbling and spattering—Liz done nursing, singing lullabies to Hannah—I moved a particularly annoying pile of dirty baby bottles and beer cans from one counter to another. I rinsed my old dull knife so that I could chop eight ounces of chanterelle mushrooms—amazingly expensive—and then sauté them in butter and . . .

"No, no, no, no," said Lisa, Alice's sometimes-lawyer. "I can't hear any more about this."

"What?"

"Ugh. It makes me sick just hearing about all those little amounts. I'm a very good cook, actually. I'm really *quite* good. But I do my own thing. I mean, I look at cookbooks for ideas, but that's it."

HOW TO COOK LIKE A MAN

Jane Kramer, writing in the *New Yorker*, describes a similar friend getting a headache "just by looking at the teaspoon measurements for thyme and garlic in a coq au vin." I believe that my mother fell into this same camp. Not that Mom ever let on: "What a fabulous idea!" Mom exclaimed, regarding my *Vegetables* project, but I caught a telltale blankness in her loving eyes, some part of Mom's mind recognizing the personality gulf between us. Cooking wasn't something she'd ever had to discover, or fret about, or explore. She simply cooked, with pleasure but without pretension. Meatloaf, cinnamon toast, spoon bread, lasagna and cheesecake for my every birthday: I recall all of this with a tingling warmth. And yet I do not recall a single cookbook ever present in our home, except an old copy of *Joy of Cooking*. Nor do I recall a single food magazine. When I think of Mom cooking even her Classy Dinner Party Beef Stew, I picture her peacefully puttering away in our puny kitchen, adding a dash of this and a drop of that, finding her way toward a great meal. None of these people, however—neither Mom, Kramer's friend, nor Alice's lawyer—had ever looked toward cookbooks for immutable laws of action during a period of intense personal disorientation. None of them had ever needed cookbook recipes to dictate the very movement of their limbs through space, minute by minute, hour upon hour, during the tense passage of a young family's no-sex, no-restaurant evenings, the future ever more daunting.

Alice herself commanded, in the *Vegetables* introduction, that I should "never cook slavishly, rigidly following a recipe and thoughtlessly adhering to the measurements it gives. . . . Trust your intuition and your own taste." But if Alice had been standing before me, wagging a finger, I would have protested to my teacher that, for a man lacking both intuition *and* taste, recipes qualify as oxygen: they make life possible, *if and only if one lives and breathes by them.* Only in following every instruction to the letter, see, could I hope to learn what the hell food was supposed to taste like in the first place. Improv is just fine if you've made tens of thousands of meals and long since learned that, say, lemon juice in a salad dressing plays the part of the acid, balancing the oil. If you've never made a salad dressing in your life, you might think that the lemon juice was all about a vaguely citrus-like flavor, and that orange juice might work, too. What would you learn then, except that you're a shitty cook who ought to follow recipes?

Clearly, I had more in common with certain other friends described by Kramer, like the Los Angeles couple who "read cookbooks aloud to each other in bed, as part of what could be called their amatory ritual" or the couple in Berlin who "nearly divorced over an argument about which cookbooks to pack for a year in Cambridge." Okay, I'm overstating it: Liz would never have seen anything amatory about reading a cookbook together, unless it happened to be Bayless, and I was diving in just to please her. But I had yet to consider a move like that. My point is just that I was closer to Kramer herself, seeing cookbooks as "like the lipsticks I used to buy as a tenth grader in a Quaker school where not even hair ribbons or colored shoelaces were permitted. They promise to transform me." And sure, while the young Kramer hungered for a ticket into the more illicit aspects of adulthood, I needed a recipe for middle age, a way to maintain a sense of self. The spirit was the same, though, and I've been consistently surprised by how few people share it.

Take my only cooking-obsessed friend, Ignazio, a midforties Italian always laughing happily at the out-of-control absurdity of his own messy but wonderful life. I didn't actually know Ignazio back when I started cooking. We met more recently, through mutual friends. But my wife likes his wife, Heather, a pretty American redhead, and their kids are close in age to our daughters. I love stepping out of the elevator in Ignazio's building into his sun-flooded third-floor apartment in North Beach, a few blocks off Fisherman's Wharf in the old Italian neighborhood. My daughters run immediately to Giovanni's room, the wives retire to the couch with a cocktail, and Ignazio and I make like modern men, heading into the room we both like most, the kitchen. Opening Ignazio's oven, I typically inhale the deep aromas of a big roast, a leg of lamb maybe, fragrant with hot thyme and rosemary, and that's when it begins, the conversation we always have.

"God, you're such a good cook," I say. "That smells *so* good."

"Oh, no, no. It's stupid, the way I cook!" Ignazio replies, in his thick Italian accent. "It's really stupid. I wish I could learn to use cookbooks the way you do, but I just don't. I don't know why I don't, but I don't. But I find it so incredibly interesting that you can use cookbooks, Dan. You're so disciplined, and you have so much patience. I don't have that patience. And your food is always so good! It's so interesting!"

To some degree, we're just acting out the new male Kabuki, dinner-party version: "Oh my God, bro, I cannot believe you've gone to *so much fucking trouble*! You are *such* an awesome cook! And you make it look so easy! My wife is just absolutely going to *fucking leave me* and move in with you!"

"No, no, no. Dude. I'm not a good cook at all. I'm a fucking shitty cook! But *you're* the best fucking cook in the world. I've told absolutely everybody at the gym about those double-thick porterhouses you grilled last time!"

And yet, there's something real at work, some genuine gulf between Ignazio and myself. Cookbook obsession, Kramer has argued, is a distinctly British and American phenomenon. Italians, by contrast, have long viewed the very owning of a cookbook—or at least any cookbook beyond a couple of culturally approved Italian culinary encyclopedias, such as *The Silver Spoon*—might carry the implication that Mama, and therefore Italy herself, had failed to pass along the heart of Italian culture. Fiorenzo Andreoli, an Italian chef quoted by Kramer, voices precisely this anti-recipe chauvinism when he says, derisively, of his time in San Francisco restaurants, that everybody he met out there "cooked with his nose in a cookbook."

I shared all these thoughts with Ignazio during our most recent meal together, over at his place. Heather, his wife, said that Ignazio's very own mother, during her semiannual San Francisco visits to hang out with the grandkids, was often viciously critical of Ignazio's cooking ("You call that pesto!? My own son!?"), as if to reassert the primacy of her own judgment, and to reinforce Ignazio's faithful understanding that Mama's cooking, the cooking of the Italian people, and the universal Good Cooking of the human race were all one and the same, inseparable. Ignazio laughed, too; we'd all had a lot to drink, and we'd eaten too much, and Ignazio takes every opportunity to be unsentimental about Italy and the Italians. He even hoped to pitch a reality TV show, he said, in which he and his mother would go around to Italian American restaurants and sample the food and say mean things. A fair-minded soul, however, Ignazio volunteered interesting evidence to support my core point: his grandfather had been a professional chef, as had many of his other male relatives, and every single dish his mother ever made was an established, time-tested part of the Milanese cultural repertoire, long since mastered by members of his own family. Every dish Ignazio had ever eaten while growing up, therefore, had come from a recipe—one handed down orally, perhaps, but a recipe nonetheless—and he'd have to have been a genuine half-wit not to have absorbed all of those recipes through the very pores of his own skin.

It's not just the Italians, either: I've also been on the receiving end of anti-recipe prejudice through a friend named Sammy, owner of the Bi-Rite Market, which happens to be my favorite San Francisco grocery store. I dropped by one day, to pick up a few things for Alice's Radish, Fennel, and Dandelion Salad, and I got distracted buying extra fennel for a few other random fennel recipes from *Chez Panisse Vegetables*—perfect examples of dishes that sounded awful to me but which I meant dutifully to make in the spirit of expanding my culinary mind. Sammy asked what the hell I needed so much fennel for, and I ended up telling him about my newfound love for cookbooks. I'd expected to bond with Sammy over this, but I learned instead that my recipe obsession conflicted so deeply with his sense of how a real man ought to behave that he laughed affectionately and said something like, "Wow, Danny, I cannot deal with recipes. I fucking *never* look at recipes." But, see, Sammy's mother—like Ignazio's—was a great cook from an ancient tradition, in Sammy's case Palestinian. Plus, Sammy himself had been a professional chef before he took over the Bi-Rite Market from his Palestinian-immigrant father; he'd gone to culinary school, he'd interned at a French restaurant in Switzerland, and he'd opened his own little San Francisco bistro at age twenty-four. Like every cook, chef, and culinary student everywhere, therefore, Sammy had followed fixed recipes many thousands of times, bringing to mind the jazz analogy: sure, it's all improvisation if you're already Wynton Marsalis, but it's improvisation on a fixed set of standards, and doesn't a guy get to learn the standards? Even if, for example, you're not really capable of simultaneously watching fennel on the backyard grill and simmering more fennel on the stove and tracking the doneness of pasta and figuring out that your Radish, Fennel, and Dandelion Salad tastes disgusting because you've bought dandelion greens so old and grown-up they have exactly one flavor: bitter? And while I got the message, yet again—Real Cooks Don't Follow Recipes—I kept right on measuring every teaspoon of parsley without self-consciousness.

To some degree, this had to do with questions non-culinary. For the goals that actually mattered—my need to bail on the Great American Novel, and to become a responsible father before Hannah discovered that I was not one—precise amounts were unavailable. Clear instructions were unimaginable. Completion, in the two or three hours before Liz freaked out with hunger and rage and poured herself a fucking bowl of cereal right in front of my face, was utterly impossible. But right up to the very last of the pasta and salad recipes in *Vegetables*, all of the above satisfactions were palpably available, and precisely because, in deciding that my own palate was stupid, I'd cleared out other considerations like, say, whether or not Liz even felt like eating Pasta with Zucchini, Walnuts, and Pesto on a given night. She'd consistently said she didn't care, during those vulnerable first months with a baby. By the time she did begin to care again, around months four and five, it was too late. I'd already developed a fierce emotional attachment to menu control, narrowing my job down to recipe completion and nothing more—as if I were building model airplanes that happened to be edible. I'd come to love that I could stop thinking and follow Alice's orders, none of which included cleaning as I cooked. Trim and julienne a little "zucchini or other summer squashes," boil noodles, *kablam*: checkmark next to the recipe's title, in the book's table of contents. Ditto with the next main-course category I tackled: pizza, even when I got flour all over my clothes and the countertops, and even when the crust came out soggy, puffy, and bready. Yeast in warm water, add flour, let rise, knead again. Then: "Preheat the oven to 375. Dice the onion and toss in a small ovenproof sauté pan with a pinch of salt and enough olive oil to coat lightly," until, two and a half hours after I'd started, the kitchen ransacked and burned food be damned, I would absolutely have achieved something a reasonable person might describe as Pizza with Broccoli Raab, Roasted Onion, and Olives.

I found yet another stripe of anti-recipe prejudice, which I will call the Lamentation of the Disappointed Cookbook Lover: "Like sex education and nuclear physics they are founded on an illusion," writes Anthony Lane, the *New Yorker*'s movie critic, of his own love for cookbooks. "They bespeak order, but they end in tears." Similar sentiment from Adam Gopnik, in the same magazine: "The anticlimax of the actual, the perpetual disappointment of the thing achieved. . . . You start with a feeling of greed, find a list of rules, assemble a bunch of ingredients, and then you have something to be greedy about. In cooking you begin with the ache and end with the object, where in most of the life of the appetites—courtship, marriage—you start with the object and end with the ache." (Gopnik skipped adolescence—there's no other way to explain a man's thinking that eros begins with a specific object of desire, and not with an aimless ache.)

Ruth Reichl leads the most visible counterattack against the Disappointed Cookbook Lovers, dismissing their pursuit of perfection and claiming to love, instead, the way no dish ever turns out the same twice, guaranteeing that Reichl's cooking will always be an adventure. "I cook for other people, and to me, cooking is an act of giving," Reichl continues. "When I leaf through cookbooks or magazines I am imagining all the people who will be sitting around my table, and I am looking for food that will make them happy." I liked the sound of this, back then; and I know that I wanted the emotional extra credit owed to anybody cooking in this spirit; but even I knew that I was cooking almost entirely for myself, hunting perfection in precisely Gopnik's spirit, horrified by the idea of culinary adventures and of dishes turning out differently, night after night. So I knew what Lane and Gopnik were talking about: recipes always sound good, but they rarely work out the way you've dreamt; words on a page cannot a chef make. And yet, even here, as with that whole Recipes Give Me a Headache ideology, I was blessedly unafflicted in the early days, because my own ache was so unrelated to food. I could no more ache for Alice's Turnip and Turnip Green Soup, to cite a dish from the subsequent soup phase (Asparagus Soup, Black Bean and Roasted Tomatillo Soup, Corn Soup with Salsa, lot of soup), than for the moons of Jupiter. The words "Turnip" and "Turnip Greens" meant nothing to me; together in a combined noun, they might as well have been Fortran. Turnips and turnip greens did sound unlikely to be worth eating, and I suppose that's at least a little bit of meaning, but it was a meaning based on suspicion, not information.

Once I'd cleared that baseless suspicion from my mind, nothing remained, allowing me to see the words "Turnip" and "Turnip Green" as they really were, for me: empty of the power to signify, much less to evoke an ache for Turnip and Turnip Green Soup. And it was precisely this emptiness of specific meaning that acted like a tonic upon my self-hating mind: it was precisely because I hadn't a clue that I could experience the quest to acquire that clue as purposeful, answering this man's immediate emotional need to spend at least one part of each day chasing tangible, useful (edible) results.

When that quest became difficult, as in the case of "2 bunches young turnips, with their greens," I found pleasure in the pursuit. Turnips may be among the most common of vegetables, available in every grocery store everywhere, but I personally had never knowingly eaten one and hadn't the vaguest idea what a turnip even looked like. So I first had to ask Liz, who did her best to describe them. Then I foolishly began my search in our neighborhood. Full of optimism, I grabbed my wallet and walked down our narrow little lane to Cortland Street, the local business district. I passed a beauty salon regionally famous for expertise in black women's hair, and the Chinese restaurant proudly displaying, in its window, a newspaper review headlined "Hunan Chef Doesn't Suck." The pet store came next, and then the neighborhood grocery. There, I found only turnips of the type I now know to be ubiquitous: dull pinkish-white tennis balls looking like they've fallen out of a garbage truck and been run over a couple of times before tumbling into the gutter. No greens involved, and therefore no end to my turnip quest.

The next Saturday, with spring finally coming to California, we all woke up early. Liz, the prior afternoon, had consumed her first latte since giving birth. Hannah, as a result, had absorbed copious coffee-spiked breast milk and slept hardly a wink. So I struggled to convince a bleary-eyed Liz that we might have fun on a family turnip mission to the Ferry Plaza Farmers Market, a place I'd not yet visited. I've since come to see this market as Mecca to the Northern California cult of fine food. Not the Innermost Temple—that lies somewhere inside the Chez Panisse kitchen, wherever Alice browbeats interns into the endless peeling of tiny fresh fava beans—but a place of pilgrimage nonetheless, hallowed ground on which aspirants practice all the skills of their worship, reaffirm commitment to certain codes and values.

Thrilled to have company, Liz and Hannah coming along for the ride, I took the freeway north, swooping over the Mission District and past downtown to the 4th Street exit. We passed underneath the Bay Bridge, where I parked along the glittering waterfront. As we walked toward the market, we joined a river of the food-obsessed affluent, a human current of the anxiously inbound (*GOT TO GET SOME FUCKING NETTLES BEFORE THEY'RE GONE!!!*). Legions of the happily outbound hustled the other way, bags bursting with baby leeks and Chioggia beets, wood-oven baguettes and live lobsters: *That's right, got mine!*

Finally, I saw the portal through which I'd have to pass to enter the market: the phalanx of sizzling, smoking restaurant booths forming an outer flank of temptation. Like baleen in the mouth of a whale, all those expertly cooked softshell-crab sandwiches, sustainable-pork BLTs and pastured-egg omelets filtered out the unserious by encouraging them to blow off shopping, eschew cooking, screw personal growth, and just buy a big, beautiful plate and settle in to chow.

I paused there a moment, looking up at the Ferry Building clock tower and the blue sky beyond. I felt my pulse accelerating. I hadn't even entered yet, and I wanted everything: I wanted to eat every bite from every booth and thus to know what all these people knew. But then I remembered the turnips with turnip greens and took the plunge. I marched straight past all the breakfast-eating amateurs and right down the throat-like corridor of the lavender-and-flower merchants into the whale's belly— the farm stands themselves. There, I found a once-in-a-millennium conglomeration of the world's most beautiful plant foods, with "dry-farmed Early Girl" tomatoes looking like the Platonic Ideal of tomato-ness, and whole plants of basil for sale cheap, and mountains of multicolored sweet peppers, and exquisitely tender frisée. The fevered crowd, swirling around me, engaged in the uniquely San Franciscan contact sport of elbowing past the chutney-buying tourists to grab the last of the jumbo levain loaves at Della Fattoria—sweating the hot sweat of panicky desire, bribing pissed-off kids with five-dollar cinnamon twists and six-dollar smoothies, and then paying way too much for a pig's liver that ought to be free, given how nasty a grown-up pig's liver typically tastes (suckling-pig organs are different). Out of the corner of my eye, in the swirling kaleidoscope of agricultural bounty, I saw a woman holding postcard-perfect French breakfast radishes up to the light, scrutinizing their flawless tender greens for the slightest signs of wilt. I remembered suddenly that *Vegetables* had a radishes chapter, and the memory made my pulse quicken even more. A bead of sweat ran down my ribs. I could see picture-perfect baby carrots—no bigger than my pinky, priced like jewels—and I could recall a recipe or two for which they'd be ideal. I could see a sign saying "Tat Tsoi," and another reading "Amaranth Greens," and both were key ingredients I'd not only never seen before but never thought I'd find as long as I lived.

Bolting to bag some radishes of my own, I wondered: *How many bunches do I need to knock off every single radish recipe tonight?* My wallet now more open than closed—Liz a little appalled, I think, to see my profligacy with our grocery dollars—I began to bounce from farmer to farmer, buying anything and everything as if my life depended on my project's completion, as if this market were the only place on earth to find the essential ingredients, as if this very Saturday might just be the market's last day ever, before the Judgment Day upon which a wrathful God might demand to know why the hell I'd not yet completed the shelling-peas section of *Vegetables*.

Then I saw them: young white turnips, smaller than golf balls, fresh green leaves truly sprouting off their tops.

A familiar voice said, "What up, double-D?"

I looked up from the turnips and, to my surprise and delight, saw a guy I'd known in a former life, a tall, unshaven, shaggy-haired surfer named Joe. The very sight of Joe's face brought a knee-weakening tide of nostalgia for weeks on a certain Baja beach, surfing all day in warm water, eating fish tacos and drinking beers at night, and sleeping blissfully with Liz, just the two of us. But Joe stood on the backside of the farm table, surrounded by several shockingly beautiful young hippie-farmer girls. So I asked what the hell he was doing in San Francisco.

"Selling turnips, man! I'm a farmer!"

Liz, speaking softly to me, said, "Sweetheart, I've got to get out of here. Hannah's melting down."

"Hold on, sweetie. Joe's got turnips. You remember Joe, don't you?"

She smiled at him. Then, to me, Liz said, "Honestly, honey, I can't deal anymore."

"Okay, okay. Just hang in a little longer." I got carried away, paying alarming prices not only for Joe's perfect Tokyo turnips, as he called them, but for the rest of his early-spring offerings, like shallots and kale, chard and carrots, even strawberries and baby leeks. I feel a measure of guilt, in hindsight, over the way I led the exhausted Liz and the screaming Hannah onward through the rest of the booths, buying up still more foods I'd seen in *Vegetables* but never in a store: savoy cabbage, escarole, curly endive. I saw astounding things for which I did not yet have recipes, and could therefore not yet rationalize the splurge: shockingly tasty cheeses; fresh fish for a small fortune per pound; locally grown beef, chicken, lamb, pork, goat, and eggs. I led my wife and baby into the Ferry Building itself, too, a vast emporium with a high domed ceiling. Like one long large intestine, the hall branched off here and there into an All-Star lineup of Northern California's very highest-status, highest-prestige local food labels, from Recchiutti Confections to Prather Ranch Meats, and from the Cowgirl Creamery to Boccalone ("Tasty Salted Pig Parts") to Far West Fungi. Sur La Table alone, the upscale kitchenware store, carried so many things I suddenly wanted to own that I had to hustle Liz and Hannah out of the building and back down the waterfront as if I'd just smoked my first pipe of crack and liked the rush so much I knew I was coming back.

After returning home, while the enraged Liz and the oblivious Hannah fell asleep together, I diced and sautéed exactly the prescribed amount of onion and garlic. Then I sliced up those costly little turnips and added them to the pot, and I then added just the right amount of bay leaf, thyme, bacon, and vegetable stock that I'd made the night before. The turnip greens went in last, around the time Liz got up from her nap. I shaved a little Parmesan onto the top of our bowls and then, precisely because I'd resisted all impulse to improvise, I liked the soup. I liked it a lot.

"This is great," Liz said, already willing to forgive. "I love this."

"I'm so glad, baby."

She smiled. "You'll never make it again, will you?"

"Never."

"And remind me why?"

"Forward motion, baby. Got to keep moving."

4
We All Need Something to Believe In

"Food—at least as much as language and religion, perhaps more so—is cultural litmus," according to Felipe Fernández-Armesto, in *Near a Thousand Tables: A History of Food*. "We continually devise ways to feed for social effect: to bond with the like-minded." Think of adolescents and their fierce interest in the finer shades of musical taste: "Well, I *know* she's like *totally* smoking hot and super sweet and ultra smart and *totally* perfect for me in every imaginable way, and she even actually likes me, which is amazing, but I'm really worried that I don't know what kind of music she listens to." And when it comes to food, it's not just the feeding: cookbooks play an outsized role, placing the food in its all-important cultural and aesthetic context, telling you what the food actually means—like Fergus Henderson's cult classic *The Whole Beast: Nose to Tail Eating*, from which I would one day cook Deviled Kidneys ("the perfect breakfast on your birthday") and Pot-Roast Half Pig's Head ("the perfect romantic supper for two"), claiming membership in a club of the unsqueamish, presenting friends with Deep-Fried Lamb's Brains and a facial expression that says, "Oh *come on, please* tell me you're not grossed out. I've *always* loved lamb's brains!" David Chang's recent *Momofuku*, too, packaged his New York restaurants' recipes in foulmouthed conversational narrative and blurry photographs of tattooed diners in cutting-edge urban street fashions—some of them secretly famous, at least in food circles—reassuring me that hours burned on making Chang's magisterial ramen would get me far more than a great bowl of food, it would even purchase entry into the hippest current clique of the like-minded.

As powerful as Chang and Henderson have been in recent years, at least among people like me, they scarcely rank next to Alice's own act of cultural litmus-creation. California State Historian Kevin Starr, recognizing her rare gift for envisioning a beautiful life and then announcing that she and her dazzling friends already led that life in a way that could make millions crave instruction on doing the same, credits her with making food-and-wine connoisseurship a key membership test for the liberal elite. "Let the rest of the country vote Republican and eat out of cans and packages," he writes, in *Coast of Dreams: California on the Edge, 1990–2003.* "Berkeley would reform the world . . . while dining on salads of dried cranberry, pecans, and arugula, free-range fowl from oak-fired ovens, fresh-baked whole-grain breads, and an appropriate white wine, with poached pears for dessert." And if anybody was a born sucker for this dream, it was me—not least because my very own Republican grandparents had proudly worn formal dinner attire to eat Continental brown-sauce dreck at their country club while I'd worn jeans and skateboarding sneakers to Chez Panisse itself, on my very first dinner date. Thirteen years old and I'd proudly led the pretty Miss Jane H. up the Chez Panisse stairs into the upstairs café, wide-eyed with wonderment at a glittering world of grown-ups. Nervous kid on a big night, I'd been absolutely thrilled to see my father's law partner, Ted, sipping wine at the tiny bar. I still recall Ted's affectionate smile, the way he leaned back and bellowed, "Hi, Danny!" so that I felt special. Ted knew how much I'd love being treated like a grown-up, out on the town, so he kindly introduced himself to Jane and then left us alone drinking water at our two-top and sharing a calzone. Hot raclette cheese melted out of that crispy crust, and I'll never forget Jane's young skin, her brilliant eyes funny and alive. And sure, the bill did come to a little over nineteen dollars, and I did foolishly imagine this meant that my single twenty-dollar bill was enough to cover the tip, but it's all a fine memory nonetheless, warm and happy and fun—and those were precisely the feelings evoked by my opening the *Chez Panisse Café Cookbook* itself, when Hannah turned one.

"After almost twenty years," Alice wrote in that book's introduction, "the Café is still a place where people hang out together, and measure out the years from Bastille Day to Bastille Day and from New Year's Eve to New Year's Eve." And look, I knew perfectly well there couldn't be a single, solitary, nondelusional, non-French soul in the entire Golden State honestly measuring out anything at all between Bastille Days. Nor was I blind to the overt salesmanship of Alice's next bit about how "my old friend, film producer Tom Luddy, still drags in every foreign director and starlet imaginable. . . . Retired professors and Nobel Prize laureates still lunch quietly, and our Saturday lunch regulars are still known by name to cooks and waiters alike." But I craved that sense of belonging and I had a perfectly reasonable membership claim to precisely this imaginary clique.

I'd also run aground a little, with *Chez Panisse Vegetables*. Having finished all the soups, salads, and pastas, I'd been looking at a hundred-plus vegetable side dishes. Liz rightly wondered, during one dinner I made for friends, why anybody outside pre-famine Ireland would serve a banquet consisting of potato pasta, potato gratin, a side of sautéed potato slices, and a platter of roasted fingerling potatoes. Unwilling to repeat dishes, I therefore needed a new raft of mains for my recipe-ticking mania. The *Chez Panisse Café Cookbook*, which I already owned, offered an obvious first step toward a solution. "We have paid special attention to the ingredients we left out of . . . *Vegetables*," Alice wrote, also in that introduction: "fish and shellfish, meat and poultry, eggs and cheese." In short, everything a man wanted to eat. Simply in broadening my mission, I realized, and redefining it as an assault on the entire Chez Panisse cookbook oeuvre, I could squeeze through this frightening little bottleneck by combining mains from the *Café* book and even others, like *Chez Panisse Cooking*, by longtime Chez Panisse chef Paul Bertolli, with all the *Vegetables* outliers. And that's how I fell truly under Alice's spell, her vision of a broader community—Paul Bertolli among its leading lights, along with various other cookbook authors—living the grand Chez Panisse lifestyle.

"One of my partners had befriended a farm family in Amador County in the Sierra foothills who kept a few hogs and who had agreed to supply us with suckling pigs," Alice writes, and so I showed up at the Marin Sun Farms booth at the Ferry Plaza Farmers Market, and I tried to befriend the poor rancher while I scored the goods for Long-Cooked Pork Shoulder, Simple Cured Pork Chops, and Roast Pork Loin with Rosemary and Fennel. Somebody named Nancy Warner and her family, according to Alice, slept outdoors "with the chickens to protect them from attacks by coyotes and roaming packs of dogs," and who wouldn't like to feel that a slumber party might replace cyanide-laced deer carcasses and government "predator control" specialists? And, thus, I bought "pastured" Marin Sun Farms chickens for Pollo al Mattone with Lemon and Garlic, Chicken Ballotine with Chanterelles, and Grilled Chicken Breasts au Poivre. Nobody made business arrangements in Alice's new/old Berkeley; they befriended people. The restaurant didn't offer anything as tawdry as seasonal specials; it just hewed to "cherished traditions" like "serving spring lambs from the Dal Porto Ranch," as if Alice and company were a big collective grail knight, bringing bourgeois fertility to blighted modern America.

Now we're really living, see, especially with Hannah crossing some developmental milestone bringing the world beyond Mommy into focus. Precocious talker and tentative walker, she took notice first of the dog, discovering that this hairy animal really was on Hannah's and Mommy's team, a part of their tribe; but next in line came the dawning awareness that a third human being lived in the house. Soon, my cuddles, once utterly useless at calming Hannah, acquired a modest but accelerating effect on her tantrums; my pancakes began to elicit a cautious interest, especially when she got me to serve the syrup on the side, in a little cream pitcher, so she could drink it all in one gulp. Thus, all the non-remunerative time required for all-*Café* dinners like Duck Legs Braised in Zinfandel, Grilled Endives with Sauce Gribiche, and Lindsey's Chocolate Cake with Sicilian Sabayon felt not like evasion—not like running from the Great American Novel I knew I'd have to abandon, sometime soon—so much as celebration, insistence on living the good domestic life right now.

If Hannah wouldn't nap, I'd learned, I could shut down my computer and put her in our white Subaru wagon and roam the nearby freeways and make up silly stories until the boredom and the motion made her doze off. Then I could park at the beach and let Hannah sleep while I lay on the warm dirty hood of the car, relieved to be free of my writing, and breathing all that sea air and feeling the cool wind and sun on my cheeks. Instead of lamenting that I wasn't out surfing, or that my stupid secret dream of becoming the next Jack Kerouac had to end, sometime soon,

I could feel this welling mysterious plenitude, a faintly throbbing satisfaction that my precious kid dreamt peacefully in my backseat, window ajar, smelling what I was smelling. And once she awakened, I could bounce her happily in my arms through Sammy's Bi-Rite Market, picking up lamb shanks for Soupe au Pistou. Days even came when I made it to the beach alone, and caught a few waves, and felt fine about cutting the session short to jump back in the car and zip home to run up the front stairs I'd built with my own hands, to push open the front door and find Hannah standing on her own two feet, neck craned back so that her bright blue eyes could gaze up toward me as if toward the noon sun as she spread her arms wide and shrieked, joyously, "Daddy!" Little Hannah shrieked that word like I was some kind of rock star, the greatest guy on earth, and it turned out she could make me feel something nobody else had ever been able to make me feel—that it didn't matter what the hell I did for a living, because fatherhood was the very *best* thing that ever could have happened in my life (and so he sang, *It took a little girl/to make a man out of me*).

More practical improvements, too, of course: no more breastfeeding, meaning I could take the occasional late-night bottle feeding, allowing Liz's sleep and state of mind to improve; a little freelance journalism, on my part, bringing in trickles of money, and thus justifying purchase of a Grade A goose liver for the *Café* book's Shaved Foie Gras and Rocket Salad. I could even see a new Golden Age dawning in which we'd one day risk leaving Hannah with a babysitter, maybe catching a movie. Liz, admittedly, leaned toward conversation-stoppers like, "Hey, baby, you *are* open to a second kid someday, right?"

"Of course. Absolutely."

"And, so, like . . . Okay, when?"

I tried to stall, delay: "What's that?" I replied. "*When* might I be open to a second kid? Hard to say. Hard to say. I guess I'd want to get our money deal squared away, okay?" But here, too, Alice had my back, her larger cast of characters offering just the right role models to put me at ease: this Paul Bertolli guy I'm talking about, that former Chez Panisse executive chef, later the owner of a great Oakland restaurant called Oliveto, now selling his up-scale salamis under the Fra' Mani brand. Bertolli spent his youth and early adulthood studying to be a professional musician, thereby demonstrating—to me, at least—how kitchen work could soothe a frustrated artist. It helped, of course, that I had a goofy personal connection to Bertolli: one of his music-school roommates had been a cousin of my mother's, a man named Blake, and the two young men had come to our home for dinner once. Soft-spoken, soulful, Italian American, Bertolli had since taken up kitchen work just to pay the rent. When music didn't pan out, cooking was all he had left. Bertolli was immediately successful in the food world—more than he'd ever been with music—but he writes with sadness about deeply missing "the quiet intensity, the emo-tional gratification, and the enduring reward of music making." For nearly a decade, Bertolli says, he "floundered . . . trying to find the metaphor in cooking that would reconcile my passion for the elegance of music with the rough kitchen work that was pull-ing me strongly." Then he got hired at Chez Panisse, where I'd already had that dinner date and where Bertolli discovered one of Alice's favorite books, Richard Olney's *The French Menu Cook-book*: "the poem that released me from turmoil," as Bertolli ex-plains. "In it, I found an artist's eye for the telling detail and for the beauty of food, and a craftsman's patience with process." It didn't hurt, for Bertolli or for myself, that Olney, too, had been a frustrated artist—shipping off to Europe as a young painter in 1951. Olney even had a great run of it: James Baldwin sat for a portrait still interesting to look at; Baldwin introduced Olney to a black American dancer who became a longtime lover. Olney cooked lunch for Henry Miller and found him unimpressive. (Olney found everybody unimpressive: "silly, pretentious drivel," he calls the writing of M. F. K. Fisher, a prose stylist compared to whom Olney, in my view, was a mere copyboy; and like the Hemingway of *A Moveable Feast*, Olney doles out special venom to all those who gave him much in life, such as James Beard, whose "selfishness and . . . willingness to use friends dishonestly knew no bounds and prompted no remorse.") Olney lunched with W. H. Auden, in those early Paris years, recalling how the great poet "pulled several small hotel-breakfast jars of honey and jams from his pockets, explaining that he always carried them with him, should the opportunity present itself, and that he liked to smear the stuff on boys' cocks and lick it off." (Olney says he declined to be smeared and that he and Auden never spoke again.) But after the painting came to naught, professionally speaking, Olney—just like Bertolli—found immense solace in food, becoming one of the great American cookbook writers of all time.

I felt heartened by these stories, evidence that a life could indeed have a successful second act. I hated giving up on fiction and all my fantasies of being that guy—that Great American Novelist—and I felt already a growing comfort in cooking as a creative outlet. But it helped immensely to know that cooking had done that job for others, and so I saddled up with renewed enthusiasm for the *Café* book's Rib Eye Steak with Marrow and Shallots, determined to feel whatever these men had felt. Not that it worked, exactly: I hadn't yet eaten marrow in a restaurant, hadn't a clue about its role in a dish; and so I didn't much like pushing that raw goop out of the bones, with my fingers, nor the way it looked so sad and nasty soaking overnight, blood leaching pink into the water. In fact, I kept reading and re-reading the recipe, to see where it said to cook the marrow. But I couldn't find anything but this business about mashing the marrow through a strainer "to make it smooth and remove any veins." And then, when it came time to cook the steak, I found myself grappling with Alice's demand for a dozen "foot-long pieces dry grapevine cuttings, each ½ inch in diameter," and I scanned the recipe for the part where she'd call the grapevine cuttings optional, but came up empty. So while I seared the rib eyes on my gas grill, and dealt with Liz's ongoing interrogating about that money-baby linkage I'd mentioned, I had to ask her, in return, for what I'd come to call one of our life-coach sessions—tête-à-têtes during which I depended on my wife to get my head screwed on straight. In this case: whether or not Liz thought I could even tick off the steak recipe in the table of contents, given that we didn't have a Cabernet Sauvignon vineyard on the back forty, and therefore couldn't just rustle up a few grapevine cuttings for the night's fire.

Slapping steaks onto our plates, I tried to interest Liz in a little cold, raw marrow smeared over the beef. No luck, and I couldn't blame her. It looked gross, and yet I hated that I felt that way, so I asked Liz if she'd lost her mind, on this baby thing. I couldn't for the life of me see why we'd rock the boat again, just as the waters had begun to settle. Liz couldn't see any Golden Age without Kid Number Two, so we fought, we screamed, we cried, we reconciled, and she pulled out the laptop, in bed, and googled real-estate listings in Oregon, turning up a Victorian so cheap we could sell our place and have almost no mortgage. I could write hopeless novels forever, she said; shit, I could even write poetry! But I told Liz I didn't want to leave Mom and Dad and my surf buddies. So, the next morning, Liz got in the backseat of our car, with Hannah, told me to drive, and we wrecked our entire Saturday looking at unaffordable houses all over the Greater Bay Area. Back home, pissed and miserable, we made a joint decision to stay put and get pregnant and let "the money" sort itself out—another way of saying we'd let Dan muddle through this no-more-novels problem on his own. Then I made a unilateral decision to learn every possible lesson embedded within Alice's recipe for duck confit.

Nicholas Lemann, in an essay placing Alice in the continuum of great English-language cookbook writers, defines first a pair of related traditions: Julia Child embodies the first, Americans going off to Europe and returning "to instruct their countrymen in refined cultural mores"; Elizabeth David personifies the latter, of Englishmen and -women returning home from semitropical lands "to persuade their countrymen to loosen up a little, to become more earthy and basic." Lemann locates Alice in the David tradition, and he's right, to a degree. Alice's food does evoke what Lemann calls "an easy, sensual, exotic Mediterranean life." And yet, Alice's role in the Berkeley of my childhood hardly amounted to telling the uptight townsmen to relax: the Summer of Love was old news before Alice even dreamt of Chez Panisse; Owsley had long since wrapped up his acid tests in the stucco tenement directly across little McGee Street from my very own home, in Berkeley's flat-lands; and the midseventies had seen enough pot plants sprouting in enough Berkeley backyards that snotty skateboarding kids like myself could hop fences and grab grass and get baked without attracting notice. So when Alice wrote—and when I read, as an adult, in the *Chez Panisse Café Cookbook*—that "traditional French farmhouse methods of preserving duck, geese, and even sausages and joints of pork, result in delicious, flavorful products that modern preserving methods cannot begin to match," she wasn't exactly invoking a looser, more sensual existence. When Alice thrilled me with the news that, at Chez Panisse, "we try to follow the old-fashioned French housewife's example and always keep a supply of duck confit on hand," she was playing a game far less like Child or David than like Yeats, after the First World War left our collective faith in God, King, Church, Science, Progress, and Civilization all dead and rotting in the trenches. Alice, in other words, like Yeats reaching back to Celtic wood-spirits and nature gods, found a soothing continuity in sentimental French farmhouse dreams. Grapevine cuttings notwithstanding, that was plenty good enough for me: all I had to do was learn, at long last, what on earth duck confit really was, and then make my grocery list not just for that one recipe but for Alice's suggested sides, including Crispy Pan-Fried Potatoes, and also for her suggested spin-off recipes, like Duck Rillettes.

And so, over to Sammy I go, carrying the *Chez Panisse Café Cookbook*, Bertolli's *Chez Panisse Cooking*, and even Olney's *Simple French Food*. Hannah came along because I now loved taking her on every errand she'd tolerate, trying to tantalize her palate with every free-sample tasting along the way. And Sammy lit up when he saw the little library in my shopping cart: he'd envisioned the Bi-Rite Market as the Chez Panisse of retail, he said, building community through local food; he'd just begun selling salamis made by Bertolli himself, working now on his own; and *Simple French Food* was, quite simply, Sam's favorite cookbook ever.

I told Sam the main thing I was looking for, and he said, "What the fuck, Danny! Of *course* I got duck legs. I got house-made confit, if you just want confit. But you want to make your own?" With his big strong chef's hands he took Hannah out of my arms and hugged and kissed her like a born pro (clearly unafflicted by my own reluctant-father bullshit) and insisted she just had to meet his own same-age daughter, Zoe.

"Best thing in the world, right?" Sammy said. "Being a dad?"

For the first time, I realized that I could answer that question with the full-throated certainty it was absolutely true for me, and that guys weren't just lying to each other when they said that kind of stuff; for the first time, I felt that welling pride of being one of *those* men, the real men, the *grown-ups who know that, despite the psychological torture of those early months, and the ongoing burdens and struggles, kids give an absolute meaning to our lives.*

I told Sammy I'd need about ten duck legs and three quarts of duck fat. Then we got to kicking around the whole concept of confit, and he gently helped me face the fact that I wasn't going to have a single confit leg ready to eat for at least twenty-four hours. I would therefore miss the immediate evening's opportunity for a recipe checkmark unless I settled on something non-confit in a big hurry. I left Hannah in Sammy's arms and flipped quick through that Bertolli book, settling on Ravioli of Chicken, Pancetta, and Browned Garlic, with Rosemary Oil, and then steeling myself to revisit the whole amateur-fucking-around-with-ravioli mistake.

Taking all these ingredients home, and handing Hannah off to Liz, I waited until Liz wasn't looking to splooge all the opaque white duck fat into a pot and melt it clear over gentle heat before adding all those duck legs. I knew she'd get upset if she saw that much high-priced fat serving only as a cooking medium, not even as food. As I worked toward completion, I spilled enough liquid duck fat to make the floor dangerously slick, so my feet were slipping around while I dumped all the beans in a big bowl to soak for Cabbage and Bean Soup with Duck Confit, to eat the next day. Then I put the duck and its fat in the oven at 250 degrees, pivoting quickly to dump exactly two cups of flour onto the counter and crack exactly two eggs onto the pile, to make my first-ever fresh pasta, before I noticed the recipe demanded an actual pasta machine. Liz, therefore, had to carry Hannah down those back stairs I'd built, past the tenants' apartment, under the crawl space, through the old basement door, and into the dankness to search out the pasta machine and bring it back up. And because she felt kind of sick, upon returning, she handed it over, and headed for the bathroom to do something mysterious.

"Honey?" Liz said, reopening the bathroom door, holding a white plastic stick in one hand.

I said, "Sweetie, I'm so sorry. I swear, I'll clean all this up. I will."

"I'm pregnant again."

5
What French Women Can Teach Us

"Cooking, preparing food, involves far more than just creating a meal for family or friends: it has to do with keeping yourself intact," writes Alice, in the *Chez Panisse Menu Cookbook*. I discovered this for myself when that latest pregnancy ran into trouble. A second sonogram went well enough, showing ten tiny fingers and toes. The sonogram tech, in that darkened little hospital room, recorded the fetus's femur length and head size and asked if we wanted to know the sex. We did, so he pointed to a little nubbin and said, "It's a boy." I pumped a fist, leaned close to the glowing screen, and thought instantly of how I'd have to get back into rock climbing, so I could take this boy climbing with my father. I hadn't been in years—a couple of friends, including a very dear one, had died by falling off cliffs, and I'd grown scared—but my father was still hard at it while I got fat exploring the earthy nostalgia of Bertolli's Grilled Fish Wrapped in Fig Leaves with Red Wine Sauce. So now my thoughts raced across the windswept springtime San Francisco Bay to my folks' place, around the overgrown side yard where I'd once dug G.I. Joe trenches and through the gate where I'd planted G.I. Joe snipers and across Mom's flower garden where I'd finally blown apart my G.I. Joes with firecrackers, and then through the flimsy wooden door of the falling-down garage. Somewhere inside, Dad still kept all the climbing gear we'd once shared, on all those trips together. I phoned him from the hospital hallway, outside the ultrasound room.

I told him he was going to have a grandson, and then I said, "Better dig out my climbing stuff after all, huh?"

"That is so funny," he replied, laughing. "I had exactly the same thought."

Soon, though, amniocentesis turned up a virus that doesn't do much harm unless a pregnant woman gets it for the first time during her second trimester, when it can trigger birth defects so severe a child spends every day of his life in an institution, unable to feed himself or learn anybody's name. My father said, "Life is fragile enough, son. Families are fragile enough. I've seen them fall apart. The young family you already have needs the best shot it can get." Our doctor, all our doctor friends, all our non-doctor friends: collectively, they quietly encouraged ending our pregnancy, and while it somehow seemed the clear choice, it felt unbearably ugly, sad, and cruel.

We had to wait two weeks for the appointment—two weeks during which Liz walked around feeling kicks that would never turn into breast-feeding. I became fixated on the apparent insta-bility of our old home's foundation, the possibility of an earth-quake dooming us to a complete loss of our house and our net worth. So I paid a friend, a structural engineer, to come confirm my fears about incipient underground weakness. When this friend said that our foundation, while old and imperfect, wasn't all that bad, I found another engineer, for a second opinion. When my second engineer said the same thing—you don't need a new foun-dation—I felt curiously defeated. So I told my second engineer to write up a plan for every imaginable earthquake-reinforcement move I could make anyway, throughout the entire basement.

I cooked, also, and something had changed: I cooked with absolute focus, and yet without mania. The simple steps toward Bertolli's Fish and Bread Soup felt soothing, steadying; the relatively rough work of his Salt Cod Hash, clearly lifted from Olney's *Simple French Food*, gave me the illusion of courage. Then, on the appointed late-spring day, we drove an hour north, past sun-beaten suburbs we'd searched for cheaper housing, among the golden grasses of a coming California summer. Liz and I spent the night in a good hotel near the hospital; we ordered room service, and I ate all of it, Liz ate nothing. We tried to watch a movie. In the morning, we met with a doctor who, in that awful obligation called "informed consent," told us these operations sometimes went badly. Women hemorrhaged, destroying their ability to reproduce and even, on occasion, dying. Liz looked sickened by the effort of holding all this together in her mind, but she demonstrated a lot more courage than I, because I knew now that I would fare poorly without her. So I went to the cafeteria to eat a crappy sandwich while awful things happened to the girl I loved, and I waited for a cell phone call saying the operation was over and that she'd come through okay. Hours passed under the fluorescent lights, watching nurses and anxious people like me, coming and going. My cell phone failed to ring, and I became apoplectic with fear. An hour later, when Liz should've been safely out of surgery for a couple of hours, I began to panic. I paced the antiseptic hallways; I read all the door signs for Radiology, Pediatric Oncology. Then I phoned the recovery ward and heard that Liz been recovering just fine for quite a while. The nurse had simply forgotten to phone.

Liz and I drove home like two normal non-pregnant people in a normal automobile on the highway. Same thing, stopping for groceries at the Bi-Rite Market, picking up odds and ends for some recipe or other: going through motions, behaving normally in the hopes of feeling that way.

Loss hits me like a depth charge bursting too deep down to ripple on the surface, so that I know only in a vague, trembling anxiety that a vacuum forms underneath, and that I will get swallowed; the anxiety, about the moment of that swallowing, becomes a problem of its own, a worsening fear of my own lack of buoyancy. I deal with that fear by hiding in unrelated thoughts—more reading, for example. The *Chez Panisse Menu Cookbook* carried quite a bibliography—the young Alice's way of positioning herself in a tradition—and I began ordering all of it. Escoffier, Fernand Point's *Ma Gastronomie*, Joyce Goldstein's (brace yourself, now, it's a long title) *Feedback: How to Cook for Increased Awareness, Relaxation, Pleasure, & Better Communication with Yourself & Those Who Eat the Food; How to Enjoy the Process as Well as the Product; How to Use the Kitchen as a Source of Nourishment: Emotional, Physical, & Sensual.* Alice wisely stroked the big contemporary food writers: Claiborne; Beard. But the title that grabbed me was Madeleine Kamman's *When French Women Cook: A Gastronomic Memoir.* Weary chuckles from the wife, sure—focused fiercely on getting pregnant and thereby putting "our loss," as we'd come to call it, behind us. Hannah was helping to keep me afloat, too, with her Daddy's a Rock Star routine, and I did my best underground, day after day, using my giant new Bosch hammer drill to bore big holes into the home's foundation, squirting epoxy into those holes, and then pounding in giant bolts, telling myself it was all vitally important to staving off collapse. Then I fell into bed with Kamman, hiding in her account of a pre–World War II French childhood and that ancient French understanding of how lovingly prepared food can offer sustenance and even pleasure in the face of horror.

Kamman's great-grandmother, for example, taking little Madeleine grocery shopping, every Sunday: "Market had replaced Mass ever since two of her sons had died in the Great War." Or her grandmother Eugénie, whose father had forbidden her to marry a childhood sweetheart because the boy had been Jewish—Eugénie had run away and never gone back, never again seen that sweetheart nor even her own father, as long as she'd lived. But Kamman traveled to Eugénie's village, as a teen, and managed to find Eugénie's long-lost sister and even the Jewish boy—now elderly, but still a bachelor, having held on to that love all his life. At a Christmas dinner, Kamman and this elderly pair share a feast of Eugénie's recipes: ham and sauerkraut, "quenelles of pheasant, a truffled chicken with *Pflütten*, covered with *foie gras*, and another chicken with quenelles and Riesling sauce."

Liz agreed that it was all unbearably beautiful and sad, and she listened while I read aloud the part about Kamman sent off to a children's home in the Alps, in October of 1939, after the Nazis had begun their westward blitz. Kamman describes it as the happiest winter of her life, befriending a gangly fourteen-year-old girl named Mimi: "Every Saturday, the dominant smell of the house was that of red wine in which either a rabbit, a hare, or a piece of pork was cooking." Warm hospitality, long brisk hikes in the cold blue air: "The valleys and mountains around Annecy," Kamman writes, became "the paradise of my life, the elected homeland of my heart, the place where, to this day, I strive to go back for emotional replenishment, where I want to go back forever." Horror ensues: the Nazis murder Mimi's parents and rape Mimi herself, leaving her pregnant, and yet the lesson for me, in my own time of grief, lay in the way Kamman ended this awful tale. Thirty years later, having moved to the United States and built a cooking school and cookbook-writing career, Kamman actually *does* go back to Annecy, where she and Mimi "shall forever be friends and talk and laugh around a plate of pear pancakes."

So our collective life goes on, not without its joys and not entirely unlike the war-ravaged Italian family described in a preface to *Chez Panisse Cooking*, from an Italian immigrant named Angelo Pellegrini. Likewise a child in Europe before and during the Second World War, Pellegrini—author of the eccentric memoir *The Unprejudiced Palate,* a book that Alice once told me ought to be called *The Prejudiced Palate*—describes a walk along the ancient Appian Way, near the Roman Coliseum. Smelling something wonderful, Pellegrini follows his nose into a depiction of the humble postwar Italian hearth that would've made Mussolini weep: a peasant mother, inside her bombed-out cottage, cooking wild mushrooms gathered by seven hungry children, Papa presumably dead. Bertolli's cuisine, Pellegrini means to say, reminds him of that magical mushroomy smell, the mother eking out relief in the darkest of times. And I knew I'd felt Pellegrini's meaning in the recipes themselves—because, yes, Bertolli found the time and the creative hunger to write hundreds of them, despite being Italian, and despite also writing in his own introduction that a recipe "can never quite tell enough nor can it thoroughly describe the ecstatic moments when the intuition, skill, and accumulated experience of the cook merge with the taste and composition of the food. . . . In this sense, cooking is not about following recipes."

Bertolli's long, thoughtful essays on various aspects of the eating life fit together into a single flamenco-like vision: "Bread," for example, effuses sentimentality and mystery, describing an Italian baker who'd been making a particular loaf for twenty years, having learned it from his father, and referring to the loaf always, every time he made it, as "the wise old man." Bertolli writes that spontaneously leavened bread "declares a personality and embodies a presence," and that bread, like wine, "is often understood to evoke something larger than itself." And so I mixed up a sourdough starter, let the flour and water grab natural bacteria from the air and begin to build a bulwark against hard times. A vinegar crock, too: dumping together the dregs of each night's wine glasses and bottles, storing them like memories in my construction-site basement (shear-walling, now, thousands upon thousands of big nails, fired into big plywood sheets, further protection against earthquakes made possible with my newly purchased air compressor and framing nail gun, tools of the serious carpenter, encouraged by Liz in the hopes they'd lift my mood, given that I refused to seek help), hoping said bacteria would convert all that alcohol into something of quiet, sustaining depth. Cured meats, hanging likewise in that dusty basement—Mason jars full of pickled things and preserves, tucked away in a canning cellar, and the puttering itself, the time underground and out of the daylight, getting by.

"Canning is anxiety in its absolute state," writes the sociologist Giralmo Sineri, as quoted in *Food Is Culture*, by Massimo Montanari, who adds that it's "also a bet on the future: 'Who would ever make marmalades if he didn't have the hope of living at least long enough to be able to eat them?'" Bertolli's recipes carried, for me, a similar melancholy spirit of fear joined to hope, or at least forbearance in hard times: his rabbit salad, for example, right around the time Liz got pregnant yet again. Ignoring the fact that rabbits are stupidly expensive in San Francisco, there was all the work of deboning the little limbs, cutting the meat into morsels, hacking up the carcass to simmer for a sauce. Then I sautéed the livers and kidneys, along with some wild mushrooms.

I hard-boiled eggs. I fritter-fried the meat morsels and then assembled the salad. I found it lovely and sad: the forest as bounty, the lonely cook wandering and gathering, eating odds and ends. I told myself I loved it, and I told myself that Liz's stomach was simply resistant to complex food. Eventually, I threw away Liz's entire portion, along with Hannah's. All that money, all that work, and I ate the remainder alone. Night after night, I'd ask Liz which of several Bertolli dishes she'd like to have, and she'd always say she did not care.

"Oh, come on," I'd reply, "just choose: red wine sausage, or stuffed quail?"

"Sweetie, I really just don't care."

"But doesn't one sound even the slightest bit better?"

"Both are okay, and so is takeout, or pasta. It's all fine."

Liz recognized before I did that my cooking had begun to fail as a coping mechanism, expressing my deterioration rather than healing it. She loved me but could not let herself get pulled down further with me. I misread this as mere unwillingness to commit to any stated desire, for that commitment might later call for gratitude. Once I'd picked a dish and cooked it, I watched Liz's face intensely for a reaction, as if everything were her fault. I could see that she liked the stuffed quail just fine, but she didn't eat much. I had to know why. What was wrong?

"Honey, I don't know. Please don't get upset. I guess I just find quail to be a little fussy," she said.

Fussy? Quail? What could be more relaxed! She reacted the same way to veal chops.

I said, "What? Why did you put down your fork?"

"Nothing."

"Come on, say it. You don't like it."

"It's just a little intense, for me."

"Intense."

"Yeah."

"It's not fucking intense. Veal is mild! That's the whole point of veal! It's milk fed!" I might also have mentioned that it was beautifully marinated and grilled to perfection.

She said, "Please, baby, I'm being honest. I just find it a little intense. Maybe because it's so big. I don't need as much meat as you."

"The sight of a big chop, on your plate. So it's an emotional reaction to the amount of meat, more than my cooking."

"That's who you married."

"This has to be some vestige of your dysfunctional childhood psychology."

"That's fine with me."

"Where you express control by refusing to eat."

"I get overwhelmed by food. I like to eat simply. I don't like food asking me to have a big reaction."

The first sonogram, around the time Hannah turned two, went okay: there was a heartbeat, at least. So we began to anticipate a so-called CVS test revealing sex and, of course, any genetic abnormalities. I coped by making Bertolli's Warm Duck Breast Salad, a dish Liz enjoyed just fine, and then I roasted two pigeons for dishes she found far less appealing: one for a salad, another for a soup. The salad followed the same approach as for the rabbit: roast the animal, drizzle the juices and fat into the dressing, sauté the heart and liver with pancetta and then chop them fine and toss them with the greens, perhaps a chanterelle or two, meat on top. ("Daddy," said my little Hannah, "I love pigeon.") The soup, however, was appalling.

Soon, we learned that we had a healthy girl on the way. Liz, far and away the more resilient of us, began to let go of our loss and love the new life in her womb. That was the beauty of getting pregnant again: the physical imperative toward hope. She told me it wasn't a choice, it didn't require willpower; it just was, and it helped assuage the agony of a life lost. I hadn't been through what Liz had been through—it can't have been as bad, being the man—but I struggled to feel buoyed in the same way. Even out surfing, under the autumn sky austere and beautiful—none of my surf buddies around, big clouds and rain over Twin Peaks and sunset light breaking through low and golden—I felt preoccupied with death, with my limited time on earth. These thoughts did become worrisome, for a while: I woke up one morning feeling so bleak and sick of myself that a picture of a semiautomatic pistol entered my mind, presenting itself as a solution. Not that I wanted to die. I knew even then there was a big difference between suicidal thoughts and suicidal actions. But my mind had crossed that line from thinking I should off my shitty self to settling on a method, and it startled me out of my stupor, turned my heart toward a determination to survive all this, pull myself together.

Driving in Berkeley, not long after, with Hannah in the rear and Liz pregnant beside her, I glimpsed a bus-stop bench and saw myself, less than ten years old, sitting on that very bench. I recalled an elderly woman commenting on my pretty hair. Nothing odd about the memory—just an instant when a kind woman said what lovely hair I had, and how it was a shame it wasn't on a girl. She'd been right, I recalled. That hair was long gone, dulled into my adult beige, but I'd had golden-red strawberry blond hair as a child, soft as silk. I did not recall feeling bothered by that woman's comment, nor creeped out. I recalled thinking she was nice. And now I was driving with my daughter who was happy and lovely, and with my wife who was now pregnant, and with the memory of that boy-who-never-was, and I'm thirty-seven years old and wanting this next pregnancy, a girl, to work out, but afraid to let myself hope. And I'm not so young, and I won't be around for all of Hannah's life because parents never are, and that's awful, and we're driving to see my mother and father, and my sister pregnant from a new-but-terrific boyfriend, and yet it's also all suffused with beauty and good fortune. So I'm seeing myself six years old, maybe eight, maybe ten, sitting on that bench with an old woman now dead for sure. Perhaps I had a skateboard, that day, and the little-boy me can't see that Subaru from the future drive past with himself at age thirty-seven looking out and starting to cry at the time gone by, the impossible speed of life. I tell Liz all this, and she's kind but isn't prone to such fanciful thinking. Then, because life is like this, I'm on my father's present-day floor for real, helping Hannah play with toys my mom has brought her, and hearing about Dad's climbing adventures. I can't believe my luck at simply getting to have a wife and daughter and sister and parents, all alive, grandparents buying toys for Hannah and being kind to her. So I tell my father that I feel like I'm on a bullet train in my own life. I'm in the dining car, maybe, and it's warm and cozy and friends are talking and they're serving foie and Sauternes but it's also moving too fast. If I glance out one window I see the face of that fetus's death, my own death (my father's death, too, though I don't tell him that), and all the photographs of children dead in their parents' arms in this South Asian tsunami that has just happened. Cancer diagnosis next week, car wreck the month after, colossal earthquake and we lose everything. Or, glance out the other window, on life's imaginary bullet train, and I'm walking on Bernal Hill at dusk with Hannah and our ridiculous dog, Sylvie, and with my visibly pregnant sweetheart,

Liz. It's winter, maybe, so the western sky glows luminescent orange behind Twin Peaks, and deep blue overhead. The city lights come up bright and sharp, the hills all outlined in black, and it's all unbearably beautiful, even if I can only be here for ten minutes before rushing home to cook dinner and give our great kid a bath and read her *Goodnight Moon* and, as ever, fall asleep on her floor, holding her tiny hand in my own. But still, there I am on Bernal Hill, holding Hannah up in my arms, pointing to a distant copse of eucalyptus trees silhouetted black on the hot orange sky. I point out these trees to Hannah because I want her to see the beauty of the world. She always does, and she says, in her soft, lovely little voice, "Can I go there someday?" The question feels like a beautiful knife in my heart. "Someday?" *Will I be around?* My own days seem so finite—knowable, countable. But now the waiter's returning with the main course, the roast chicken or pepper steak with a different wine pairing, and different friends are joining us, and if we don't glance out the window we won't see death. We won't see the guarantee of loss and suffering, and yet we won't see the aching beauty of the world, either. Maybe that's fine, I'm telling my father. Maybe it's okay to keep the dinner table so full of friends that only occasional over-the-shoulder glimpses-out-the-window even tempt you, and even then only in fleeting reflexes, so that about the time you've even noticed the death's-head in the clouds or the haunting warmth of the harvest moon, you've already snapped back to hear what somebody's telling you about Bordeaux futures, or the new butcher shop in Hayes Valley. Not that food or wine can make any genuine pain go away, or lift the burden of the past. But it turns out they can help a little, if you know the right tricks, and that counts for something.

6
The Happy Hunting Ground

Heaven on earth, eternal sensory pleasure taken from the creation itself, in one long Edenic orgy among the organic apple trees: read Alice's cookbooks closely enough, and with enough wide-eyed yearning, and the core Chez Panisse dream comes to look very much like this. It's as if the pain of history, the toxic impurity of the mechanized present, and even the tragedies awaiting every one of us, in the passage of time, might fade to pink in the soft worship of a tongue savoring a peach at the height of ripeness, a late-summer's tomato drizzled with good local olive oil, a line-caught California King salmon grilled in fig leaves on a redwood deck overlooking a sublime Pacific Ocean sunset among sophisticated wine-loving surfer friends equally skilled at oyster shucking, locating the G-spot, and selecting the right vintage of California cult Cabernet Sauvignon to go with herb-crusted Sonoma county rack of lamb and rosemary-garlic new potatoes. Nothing new about this, either—truly timeless human aches for simpler worlds in which the forest might always teem with game, the hedgerow with berries, the creek with fish, the Happy Hunting Ground of certain Native American traditions.

I found myself drawn to these dreams in the period of my recovery from that loss, beginning with a magazine assignment that got me on a plane to Anchorage, Alaska, and then out to Homer, and then onto a hired motorboat headed for a fishing lodge. Once we'd loaded my luggage, that boat ferried me through Homer's little marina, past storm-battered Bering Sea crab boats moored alongside beaten-up purse-seiners and long-liners with dented aluminum bait shacks. We entered the open waters of Kachemak Bay, cruising below giant ice-covered mountains and rivers draining through sweeping spruce forests, past rocks roaring with the squawks of ten thousand seabirds, alongside sea lions and otters and kelp beds. I disembarked at a private little dock and carried my bags into the Kachemak Bay Wilderness Lodge, where I'd booked a private cottage perched among evergreens on a sunny bluff over the bright blue estuary.

I'd come for the salmon fishing, but I'd never been much of a hook-and-bullet guy. So I got a morning clinic from a guide named Josiah, a burly New Englander with a Moby Dick tattoo on his forearm. Then Josiah revved up the outboard on a Boston Whaler and took me into the glassy-flat waters of China Poot Bay. Eagles sat in the big Sitka spruce. Bears wandered along vast, vacant cobblestone beaches. Pink salmon schooled below the boat, heading inland to spawn and die. Josiah did everything, baiting my hook and casting my lure and getting a big, gorgeous fish on the line. The silver salmon rocketed away from the boat, zipping out the reel. Josiah handed me the rod and said, "Okay, when he turns back toward us, be ready. Reel in fast."

I held the rod's tip up, keeping the hook in the salmon's lip. Josiah grabbed the net and leaned his barrel chest against the gunwale, ready to scoop. The salmon shot off to one side, then to the other. Then it bolted straight away, knifing my taut line through that mirror surface.

"Damn, look at that," Josiah said. A dozen sea lions had just rolled off a sandbar. They swam toward us. "It's hard to compete with two million years of evolution," Josiah said. "Don't lose this fish, because there won't be any left when those guys get here."

I stumbled for balance as the fish made another run toward me and then hauled into a U-turn, showing us a broadside of its long body. Josiah sensed a yielding, so he had me pull the fish back toward us, wearing it down. Then Josiah stuck out his thick Moby Dick arm and scooped up fifteen pounds of shining, writhing salmon. He pierced the salmon's heart with a knife and blood gurgled out. We motored back toward the lodge so that Josiah could teach me how to gut it and then preserve it for the flight back to California. While Josiah concentrated on driving the boat, I thought about the seals and the bears and the eagles already eating their share of the fish all around. I said, "Hey, Josiah, what exactly are those crabs I'm seeing?"

"Just Dungeness."

Right. Just Dungeness. "And is that seaweed edible?"

He stopped the boat so I could reel in a head of emerald greenery that was not only tender, toothsome, and delicately flavored but, because we were in a tidal interface of clean seawater and pure mountain stream water, perfectly seasoned.

"While we're at it, Josiah, I'm noticing an awful lot of urchin down there on the bottom, like that sea otter keeps eating. They aren't by any chance . . ."

Soon I'd sunk an arm dragging Josiah's net on the bottom, bringing up bristly orbs. Josiah cracked them with his Leatherman. We scooped out sweet, creamy orange *uni*, discovering what the stuff in sushi restaurants is *supposed* to taste like. Fernández-Armesto, in *Near a Thousand Tables*, celebrates the oyster as the closest anybody comes to a genuinely natural food, untainted by commercial breeding and typically eaten uncooked and alive, linking us to the most ancient of paleo-human oyster eaters. Equally true of urchin, a way to slurp that pure taste of the sea.

Once ashore, Josiah had me slit the big salmon's belly and pull out its entrails. He pointed out egg sacs, bright pink: yep, like you can buy in a store, sold salted, salmon caviar. One of those big eagles sat nearby, in a spruce, waiting for my leftovers. This made me feel possessive, so I slipped the eggs into my mouth—sweet and saline, popping between my teeth. I tossed the guts onto the rocks. After a shower and a change of clothes in my cottage, I joined the other lodge guests for local oysters and blue mussels, flicking all the empty shells off the sun-bathed dock and back into the bay from whence they'd come. Word had it that a pair of eagle chicks could easily be seen in a big tree overhanging a nearby beach. So I stumbled into the woods after dinner, into the sweet golden glow of the long dusk. I found those chicks laughably huge, in a gargantuan nest. Then my attention wandered: the forest around me was a wild berry patch. In the space of an hour, I picked and ate bright, tart elderberries, salmon-colored salmon berries, high-bush cranberries and service berries and watermelon berries, and all that before I discovered a raspberry thicket. A few sheets to the wind from all the wine I'd drunk with mussels, I leaned hard against a log-pole railing the staff had built along the path.

Stretching again and again to grab yet another especially plump berry, I was reaching for what must have been my thirtieth when the whole railing broke. I fell flat on my back, unharmed. As I lay there, pulling branches down toward my mouth, plucking off the berries with my tongue, I knew that I had tasted a vision of heaven— not just because the raspberries were so good, but because the whole picture, including all the *uni* and the salmon and the rest, corresponded so closely to the oldest human dreams of an abun-

dant afterlife, a perfect world made by the gods for human sustenance. I knew also that I had tasted a core aspect of the Chez
Panisse dream, the very one Alice evokes in *Vegetables* when she
describes the early days of the restaurant with "eccentric foragers"
arriving at the back door with "baskets of chanterelles and morels,
buckets of Pacific mussels, blackberries from the hills, and fish just
hours out of the sea."

The daily life of the modern Bay Area resident, commuting
by freeway and shopping in supermarkets like everybody else,
does not much feel this way; but that was a part of Alice's power,
her gift. By saying it was so, she helped the rest of us believe. In
believing, we felt better about our place in the world, or at least
hopeful that we *would* feel better, if we hewed long enough to
Alice's example. Upon my return from Alaska, therefore, I felt
convinced that I had broken through some film toward the mi-
raculous life available in the natural world of the West Coast. I
became determined to replicate the experience at home, in those
last months before Audrey's birth. So I started with the easy parts:
Hannah in the kid-carrier backpack, Sylvie on a leash, up that
steep Bernal Hill and into the deep blackberry brambles. Edge of
the metropolis, as if the countryside began right there; cool mar-
itime breeze blowing through hot sunshine on the golden California straw, color of the West, fog bank's misty blanket pulling
itself across the distant skyscrapers. Few wildflowers remained,
poppies curling up tight against the breeze, and Hannah loved
that she could call out their names. Little kestrels hunting on the
wing, red-tailed hawks harassed by an aggressive crow—looping
and soaring, parting and rejoining. Sylvie did her usual deal of
running off uncontrolled all over the hill, terrorizing birds, while
I placed my daughter in the dirt and found a crazy profusion of
super-ripe berries all around me, as though nobody had ever been

here, despite trashy evidence that somebody homeless made this patch a nightly bed. I wore a cowboy hat against the sun, and a long-sleeved shirt, and I stood up against this big bush, pulling down huge, swollen, ripe berries and saying to Hannah, "Okay, I need the mouth!"

"The mouth's ready!" she'd reply, and I'd place a berry on her tiny tongue, both of us all-over stained with juice.

"Mouth's ready for another!" she'd cry happily.

Plop: yet another, onto the tongue.

"Hold me, Daddy!"

I replied, quoting: "Hold me, Daddy?"

"Hold me."

Slinging her up, I kept picking with the other hand, overcome by greediness—for berries in their fleeting ripeness, and also for life, in same. Shapes of surprising experience entirely new, satisfying, not so complicated, temporarily liberated from worries about status, or money, or whatever came next. The big hawks looped in a high wind; crows did likewise; Hannah joined me deeper in a thicket, no choice in the matter, thorns at our skin and sun scorching our noses and berries ripe-to-bursting all around. I hadn't surfed in months; I hadn't exercised in weeks; but at least I was picking blackberries, telling myself it counted because the berries were ripe and if I didn't pick every single one that very day they might all fall off and rot.

Everybody's life feels fragmented, in one way or another: the friends we loved in high school, but never see; the sports we played for years; the identities dropped along the way. And many of us find pleasure in stitching those fragments together—much as I did in all that fishing and foraging. The great joys of my twenties had come almost entirely from the natural world, the Pacific Ocean in particular. So I felt as if coming home to myself when I tried, say, abalone diving, north of the Golden Gate. Abalone were still plentiful in California back when I was a kid, every Berkeley backyard fence bearing a few of those big pearlescent shells. Berkeley children grew up hearing about dads "ab diving," and I'd kept on hearing about it throughout my surfing years. But now it felt irresistible, a key part of that California-Edenic dream.

An old graduate-school friend, a former Navy SEAL named Mark, did it all the time. So I asked to meet him one morning on the Sonoma coast. He showed me how to pile all my free-diving gear onto a boogie board. Then I followed him in a long, kicking swim with flippers to an offshore kelp bed. We tied our boogie boards to heavy kelp stems, the sea cliffs about a quarter mile behind us. Then he cleared his dive mask, took a deep breath, and vanished. When I put on my own face mask and looked underwater, I couldn't see more than six feet in the frigid gray-green gloom, and the ocean bottom was apparently much deeper than that. *Not on your life*, I thought, at first. *Not on your life am I going to hold my breath and dive into that murk, with no clue what's down there.* I swam over to a particularly big mass of kelp and tried to float in the middle of it—the aquatic version of hiding behind a bush. But I was wearing a weight belt, so I could barely tread water, and my flippers kept getting tangled in the weeds.

Mark popped up holding a barnacle-encrusted disk that must have been nine inches across. He was smiling and relaxed, not at all winded.

"You swear you'll follow me down?" I asked.

"The whole way," he said.

"The whole way?"

Mark nodded—he's a great guy—so I took a deep breath, turned upside down, and started kicking. Shooting downward with surprising speed, I focused on the small field of green around my eyes. That green darkened, and then I got too scared and spun around and beat it back to the surface. I tried again, with Mark following: breathe deep, flip over, shoot down, hit the panic point (*Alert! Alert! You must turn back!*), rocket back up. Brushing through a mass of kelp, this time, I felt a rush of panic, but then I was in the fresh air again, gasping.

On my third try, I made it twenty-five feet down before a great darkness approached from below—the ocean bottom, absorbing light. Then I got close enough to see the bottom: rock reef, seaweeds, kelp anchors, this deeply hidden little universe thriving in the frigid opacity of the sea. Invertebrates clung to the rocks all around, gorgeous little creatures, and yet I had no sense of the larger topography—was this a boulder I was looking at? The edge of an abyss? The bottom of a canyon? A shark or even a whale could've been ten feet off, and I wouldn't have known it. I was already succumbing to my claustrophobia when I saw an abalone: a big round shell stuck to a rock. Flicking it off before it could seize the reef, I grabbed it, paused to look upward—the surface was only a distant haze of faint light—tucked the creature under an arm, and swam.

Home again, that afternoon, I felt more alive than I'd felt since Hannah's birth; closer to my younger self than I'd thought possible. But I felt something new, too, richer emotions available only because of marriage and fatherhood: the pride and joy of strolling in my own front door, seeing tiny Hannah explode with joy: "Daddy!" I dropped my ice chest and grabbed Hannah up off the floor and kissed her. Then I spread my hubcap-sized mollusks on the table, for all the family to see. I'd been scared witless, is the truth, twenty-five feet beneath the surf, but I craved feelings like those; I got a plain, simple, indisputable satisfaction from telling my pregnant wife and daughter how I'd swum down to the bottom of the sea and pried up dinner. Even the gory process of cutting out the guts, like I'd learned from Mark, made me feel competent in a gloriously archaic way. I loved knowing the very thing known by early San Franciscans and Native Californians before them—that to render my abalone edible, I'd have to slice that tough white meat into thin rounds, pound it toward tenderness, maybe bread and fry it. Or boil it up as a chowder, the preferred technique of San Francisco's original Bohemian crowd, led by a long-forgotten but then-famous poet named George Sterling, author of the great "Abalone Song": "Oh, some folks boast of quail on toast, because they think it's tony, but I'm content to owe my rent, and live on abalone!"

I loved showing Hannah the pretty inside of the shells, too, imagining that she and her sister-to-be might each keep one all their lives. I told Liz to call up our friends Kate and Jamie—we had about five total pounds of meat, so why not share? It was a beautiful warm night with the back door open and the sky purple over distant Mount Diablo; I still felt the fresh thrill of cold-water diving on my skin and in each deep breath; and with good wine and the stars coming out, I felt immensely happy and somehow at home, as if everything made sense, everything about the young man I'd once been, the middle-aged father I couldn't stop becoming.

7
On the Role of the Menu in Human Affairs

The first great blow to my cooking confidence emerged from the *Chez Panisse Menu Cookbook*, which also happened to be the first book Alice ever published and the last of her books that I ever tried to complete. Liz was quite pregnant by then, and I'd already begun entertaining three or four nights per week, inviting everybody we knew for dinner, as often as they would come. It's hard to believe in hindsight: with Hannah not yet three years old, and Liz carrying all that extra weight and needing all that extra sleep, and with our family finances only beginning to stabilize, I went on a dinner-party tear that would have left me desperate with exhaustion at any other time in my life. Plus, I still put a premium on maximizing the sheer number of recipes I could tackle in a given night. And I still did not see any point in cleaning as I cooked, preferring to tackle every single messy pot, pan, and spatula at the night's end, when I was often plastered. As a result, those meals were remarkably chaotic, messy, and excessive. But they weren't bad—especially when I cooked from Bertolli's *Chez Panisse Cooking*, which I'd grown to love. My mother and father came for Bertolli's masterful Fish and Shellfish Soup, a grand sort of California bouillabaisse, and they returned with friends for Veal Meatballs with Artichokes, Tomatoes, Green Olives, and Sage. I loved the role of the host, experimenting with five or six different new dishes at a time—twenty to thirty per week—in a mad, frantic rush toward I knew not what. I loved being at the center of the room, the heart of the action, whirling and spinning and heating and chopping. I'd begun writing about wine, too, so I had a lot of open bottles and I'd discovered that if I put out, say, a dozen Pinot Noirs from different parts of California, with maybe two dozen glasses for a grand total of six guests, and if I told everybody to help me sort out the regional differences in flavor profile, they'd all get drunk. And if I then presented four different varieties of shucked oysters and said everybody ought to compare and contrast, and do the same with a plate of Bertolli's own *salumi*, from this new company he'd started, and if I then hit them with a pile of whole Monterey Bay sardines fresh off my back-porch grill, and if I showed everybody how to pick up the whole fish and suck the meat right off the skeleton and then discard the head and guts, everybody would get a little disoriented and begin stuffing themselves even before we sat down to the bone-in pork loin roast and the pancetta-wrapped figs and the creamy polenta. I'd get stuffed and disoriented, too, while Liz dealt with Hannah. When the very last of the guests had gone, I'd stay up cleaning for hours and then feel our bed's mattress moving in odd, uneven circles, as if floating on a whirlpool.

Even now, I'm impressed by how supportive Liz was through that period. She's an introvert by nature, finding social life more exhausting than exhilarating. But our dinner guests were mostly old friends of hers, so that helped. She knew also that my relentless entertaining was a means of fighting back against all we'd been through, a way to embrace life and insist upon a good time. So Liz meant only to encourage restraint—a move toward less destructive evenings—when she suggested I learn a little about menu composition, constructing our evenings not just for maximum drunkenness, stuffed-ness, and recipe completion, but for perfect enjoyment. Through her own mother, Liz had a deep grounding in the core principles of hospitality: she knew that a great dinner party had to reflect the exact mood of the occasion, even one's relationship to each of the guests. I found these suggestions meddlesome at first—if I caved even a little, I feared, I would lose control over my forward progress.

That's how the *Chez Panisse Menu Cookbook* caught my eye. I'd long assumed it to be the authoritative manual for the white-tablecloth cuisine of the formal dining room, and therefore a natural someday destination in my journey, a peak I'd have to climb. But I'd noticed that, in homage to Olney's *The French Menu Cookbook*, Alice had arranged her recipes entirely in complete menus, meaning I'd have to prepare them in complete menus if I wanted to master the book's core teachings. I'd also recognized early that I would have to spend a week and several hundred dollars to prepare any single one of the menus by myself—a bridge too far, even for me. But now, I saw an opportunity—taking on these ridiculously elaborate meals under the guise of bending, for the first time, to the will of my wife. Plus, I saw a solution to the problem of time and expense: perhaps our friends would consider tackling a menu with me, in potluck fashion.

When they agreed, I gave out assignments. My buddy Rich, a handsome competitive cyclist and pharmaceuticals salesman, boned out an entire five-pound duck, lined a loaf pan with its skin, and then filled that pan with a mixture of the duck's fat, ground leg meat, and sliced breast meat, along with ground salt pork, two eggs, Cognac, and copious herbs and spices, for Duck Pâté with Pistachio Nuts. Liz's dear, close friend Kate, a pickup-basketball enthusiast and sustainable-energy expert, agreed to host the evening. She and her boyfriend, Jamie, a polymath software designer, yanked out all the guts from many pounds of Monterey Bay squid, snipped off the tentacles and cut the bodies into rings, and then sauteed all that squid with Cognac flaming in the pan. They used red wine to deglaze the pan, and then they added herbs and aromatic vegetables and set the whole thing to simmer for an hour. For my part, I spent a small fortune on several large racks of lamb. Then I marinated them in wine, herbs, and olive oil while I went through the intense drama of making my first proper lamb stock and then reducing it to a demi-glace for the sauce. Finally, for dessert, a hard-living liquor executive named Jon provided all the Sauternes for an Olive Oil and Sauternes Cake prepared by Kate, who happens to be a sensational baker.

I don't remember much about the actual evening, except that Hannah fell asleep on Kate's bed and everybody had fun, especially Liz. I felt a warm, happy glow that night, as if a grand new chapter were opening in my life. About a month later, I proposed that we all try a second menu based on an expensive ingredient I was about to acquire in quantity. I'd been offered a freelance assignment to write about foraging wild truffles in the Oregon forest. I knew that European truffles cost almost two thousand dollars a pound, so I considered this to be the only opportunity I would ever get for tackling the "Truffle Menu" of Eggs Cooked with Truffles, Crayfish Salad, Filet of Beef Lucien Tendret completely stuffed with truffles, Pommes Anna, and Raw Milk Camembert. And while our friends had mostly seen that first menu as an exhausting one-off, a crazy lark of a thing to do at Dan's behest, they were unable to resist my new setup, the promise of such a rare culinary experience.

Liz was about a week short of eight months pregnant, in early April, when we all set a date and I flew alone to Portland to procure the goods. I drove south to a restored-Victorian inn amidst the vineyards of the Willamette Valley. There, I met a gloriously plump country chef named Jack Czarnecki, author of *Joe's Book of Mushroom Cookery, A Cook's Book of Mushrooms*, and the *Portobello Cookbook*. Building a reputation and a culinary style around his unlimited access to wild Oregon mushrooms, Czarnecki had become the world's chief booster of the wild Oregon truffle. Brimming with pride, he told me that truffles were, in essence, mushrooms that had abandoned the standard evolutionary adaptation of the aboveground mushroom stem, as a means to reproduction. Growing parasitically on the root-tips of trees, truffles mature well underground. Then, when the time is right, and when most mushrooms would shoot up a stem to spread their spores on the wind, truffles release only a volatile oil that rises up through dirt and carries onto the wind a molecule precisely replicating a mammalian sex hormone found, among other places, in the urine of pregnant women. Strange miracles, but miracles nonetheless: that fungally synthesized copy of our own pheromones slips into the noses of passing squirrels, deer, and people, hijacking our brains to make us dig up the truffles, eat them with a sense of ecstasy, and then defecate truffle spores all over the woods, spawning still more truffles and still more ecstasy. It really is nice to have our brains hijacked in this way; it's a genuine marvel that an organism evolved to be sensationally delicious through that curious pathway of our sexuality, instead of the typical pathways of sugar, salt, or fat. It is precisely this that makes truffles so magical, as a food: they smell and taste like a mysterious and vaguely unclean sexual musk we cannot help craving and loving, unless we happen to *be* very pregnant women, in which case they seem to make us want to vomit, at least if we happen also to be Liz. But it is precisely this solvent-like off-gassing quality in truffles that requires, on the part of the cook and the eater, a quality I've never had in much quantity: self-restraint.

Czarnecki led me to an outdoor table set for a truffle lunch with a few other foragers, opening bottles of Willamette Valley Chardonnay and serving big plates of fettuccine Alfredo not with a few truffle specks, nor even with a judicious shaving on top, but with a sizable midplate mound of multiple whole Oregon white truffles piled up like potatoes. Thinking this a gift from the gods, I dug in, eating an entire white truffle in a single bite. I ate perhaps eight ounces by the time we climbed into cars to go foraging, and I did notice the odd truffle burp—less like garlic burps than, say, gasoline burps. But this is what I mean about monomania running me off course: determined to enjoy myself, or at least to believe that I was enjoying myself, I kept my nausea quiet as we followed a crack forager, his blind wife, and their dog into a forest everybody called the Left Nut Patch because some guy named Carl had once threatened to cut off some other guy's left nut if he ever caught the guy foraging truffles there. A filthy pair of forest dwellers appeared, and I felt a momentary fear that we'd found Carl himself. But it turned out to be two hippie meth-heads, pale and sallow, dressed in dark, damp cotton and truffle hunting for the spare change. The man wore work boots, but the woman walked barefoot.

A friend of Czarnecki's, a man named Charlie, called this woman the Girl of the Forest. He considered her mystically gifted at the finding of buried truffles.

"What's your secret?" I asked her.

"She won't tell you her secret," Charlie said.

"It's feel," said the Girl of the Forest.

Her man, admiring, said, "Sifting her duff is a waste of time."

They walked off.

I soon gathered a general conviction that our own forager's blind wife had the same mystical gift, so I followed her meandering path among the trees. Suddenly she stopped and said, "Hey, do you smell that?"

"Oh, I do! I do!"

"They must be right here!"

I smelled it, too, among the dominant cedar-and-pine aromas: an unmistakably fruity musk, a visceral sweetness. Moments later, Czarnecki dug the day's first, a big Oregon black, looking like a golf-ball-sized turd.

"Any special treat—fresh tomatoes or suckling pig—whose arrival you welcome can be cause for a special meal or a celebration of the season, any season," Alice writes, in the *Chez Panisse Menu Cookbook*. "The pungency that permeates the kitchen whenever fresh truffles arrive . . . is incentive enough to build an entire meal around those delectable fungi." I so loved the sound of this, and I so dearly wanted to live in precisely the way Alice told me to live, that I fairly trembled with excitement as the truffles piled up and the foragers packed them into bags, to send home with me. I kept it in mind that night, too, when a local Oregon restaurant turned out a many-course truffle-intensive tasting menu that, despite being delicious, left me alone in my hotel bathroom, sweating truffle stink naked on the cold floor with my slimy hand rammed down my truffled throat, desperately failing to puke. I even kept it in mind back home, packing five pounds—that's right, *five pounds*—of fresh truffles into my refrigerator. Unwilling to waste even a second, with a few days yet remaining before the planned truffle potluck, I bided my time by ticking off every truffle recipe ever published in any Chez Panisse cookbook, from eggs to pizza to chicken breasts and even salads.

I kept this up when Liz's belly once again measured too small, accompanied by high blood pressure indicating the repeat onset of that potentially fatal preeclampsia. Kate sent around a perfectly sensible e-mail wondering if we ought not postpone, and yet, because I'd now officially lost my way, I responded with a plaintive plea that our show go on, and that we'd never come into such a truffle windfall again, as long as we lived. I said that we must not give up on living and loving just because a baby was about to be born. I swore to Kate, over the telephone, right from Liz's ob-gyn hospital room, that Liz and I had everything completely under control. Then I got off the phone while the anesthesiologist injected Liz with a so-called epidural—a spinal anesthetic. The doctors and nurse left and Liz's eyes rolled back and she fell unconscious and limp off the hospital bed like maybe she was dying on the spot. I caught her lifeless body myself, before she impacted the hard floor, and I screamed and two nurses came running and one told the other to grab the oxygen mask but the other replied that the oxygen hose *had no mask*, and so I screamed at her to *get a motherfucking mask*.

Liz had only fainted. Kate soon called to say that Rich would host the meal *and* tackle the main course, so that I could focus on Liz. Within an hour of this conversation, our second daughter was born: Audrey, hale and healthy despite the circumstances. I felt calm and happy about her existence, like a normal dad, but I felt also a quiet thrill about that impending meal.

Nurses moved us to a recuperation room, and Liz said of Audrey, "She's so beautiful I could die."

"I know, baby."

When I finally brought Hannah to meet her new sister, Liz said to Hannah, "Hey sweetie, are you okay? Do you know that

I love you and that I think your sister is *so, so* lucky to have a big sister like you to help her learn everything and that we all need to be together forever and ever?"

Hannah said, "Why her name's Audrey?"

"What do you mean?"

"Why her name's *that*?"

"Ah . . . well, that's the weird thing about names, honey. Mommies and daddies just get to choose them, and that's the one we chose, and . . ."

I spoke up: "Quick question, sweetheart. About tonight . . ."

"It's fine."

"Well, no, okay. See, what I was actually thinking was that you probably need to sleep a lot and I'm worried it might be hard on Hannah and maybe she and I should sleep at home and . . ."

"Honestly, it's fine."

"What's fine?"

"Go to the truffle thing. It's okay."

"I don't have to."

"Please."

"Honestly, it's not that important, I'm just saying that . . ."

Even at the party, I couldn't leave well enough alone. Kate and Jamie had already "truffled" two dozen high-priced farm eggs by sealing them, whole and unbroken, in a Tupperware with several raw truffles. They'd melted half a pound of butter and then slow-scrambled all those eggs with half a cup of heavy cream and, because I said that the recipe's recommended two whole truffles appeared unnecessarily stingy, given my haul, with about six of those powerfully scented musk bombs. Friends named Leslie and Clara spent a minor fortune on a hundred live crayfish, poaching them in a vast vat of the first court bouillon they'd ever seen, making a sauce from the crayfish shells and a combination of

Armagnac and white wine. Rich, meanwhile, must have mort-gaged the house to buy those two whole dry-aged Prime filets of beef. Game as ever, he slit them open and stuffed them with, again, a quadruple portion of the recipe's recommended truffle allotment, along with Niçoise olives, chanterelle mushrooms, and pistachios. Caitlyn had to handle their son, Aiden, all afternoon while Rich built a suitable backyard grill to handle all that meat. And yet, despite the trouble to which everyone had gone, and despite even my own experience in Oregon—a dark secret I kept to myself—I insisted that we whip up a big batch of black-truffle ice cream, too, just because we could, and that we follow that ice cream with black-truffle whipped-cream topping for our post-meal coffee. And that's how, instead of just joining a group of friends in having fun, I pushed them all off the same cliff from which I'd tumbled myself, down toward a kind of Toxic Truffle Shock Syndrome in which too much of a good thing makes that gassy, musky truffle stink emanate for weeks from one's breath, sweat, pores, clothes, and even hair, creating a frantic yearning never again to eat a truffle as long as one lives. (Ten years later, every single one of these good people still tells me they feel a vomit-like lurch in the larynx at even the slightest smell of that distinctive truffle odor.)

If I'd read the *Chez Panisse Menu Cookbook* more carefully back then—and if I'd learned a little more about it, instead of just pushing onward with still more menus—I might have stopped the madness. I might have recognized that I was tackling the wrong book at the wrong moment in my life, and that it was high time I started asking how cooking might support the emotional core of my family's life, instead of just offering me an outlet. Like a sprawling first novel from a grand talent, the *Chez Panisse Menu Cookbook* carried everywhere the marks of ambition and enthusiasm, right down to a vast bibliography thrown in for no better reason than to show off Alice's influences and to situate her in a tradition alongside, say, Brillat-Savarin, whom she doubtless loved for such finery as "Animals feed themselves; men eat; but only wise men know the art of eating." Worse still, Alice expressed open approval, in an early chapter, for Marcel Rouff's classic 1924 gastronomic novel, *The Passionate Epicure*. It's a beautifully written book, widely admired for its depiction of a fictional nineteenth-century gourmand named Dodin-Bouffant, "the Napoleon of gourmets, the Beethoven of cooking, the Shakespeare of the table." But the novel opens with the supposedly tragic death of Dodin-Bouffant's beloved home cook, a woman who has long lavished upon her lord's guests "the rarest of sensations, the most thrilling experiences; she had exalted them, blissful souls, to the highest peaks of cloudless joy . . . wrenched cooking away from the materialistic sphere to raise it, sovereign and absolute, to the most transcendent regions which humanity can envisage." The book's early action, therefore, covers Dodin-Bouffant's intense grief not for a lost friend and human being, but rather for a key tool of his self-expression and self-pleasuring. Next comes the painful process of hiring a suitable replacement and, soon after, a competitive exchange of dinner parties with the "Prince of Eurasia," from which Dodin-Bouffant emerges triumphant, having proven himself vastly more discriminating and skilled in the pleasures of the palate. The Prince strikes back by trying to hire away the new cook. Dodin-Bouffant counters by marrying her, once again not from love but in pure commitment to gastronomy. But then Dodin-Bouffant receives seduction letters from some mysterious female admirer. Existential agony, French style: reluctant to betray his wedding vows, Dodin-Bouffant finds the sound of an erotic dalliance too much to resist. So he accepts the woman's invitation to lunch and finds her so beautiful that he tells himself he will sleep with her if her luncheon is even barely adequate. Much to his surprise, her food is in fact so masterful that he must forgo sleeping with her *for that reason*: sex would only betray his profound admiration for this woman's culinary genius.

So here's the astonishing part: the young Alice Waters, the very author of the *Chez Panisse Menu Cookbook*, takes all this seriously. I mean that: "More than any other quality in other cooks, the one I most value is the ability to see precisely what is needed in a particular dish, dinner, or event," she writes, citing Dodin-Bouffant as the very epitome of this ability to discern and discriminate. "Everything in his life was tied in to gastronomic enjoyment," she notes, describing his marvelous attention to such finer points as the "lush greenness and scent of a freshly mowed lawn" outside the dining room window, the exact number of guests required for optimal enjoyment (eight), even the precise dining-room temperature (16 degrees Centigrade). To be fair, these are perfectly appropriate considerations for a young *restauratrice*, and she was in fine company, vis-à-vis Rouff. Jeffrey Steingarten, writing an introduction to the edition I bought in paperback, shares Alice's inclination toward taking Rouff's book at face value—in Steingarten's case, by reading it as earnest argument for the redemption of classical gastronomy from accusations of gluttony. Rouff's covert purpose, as Steingarten sees it, is to build a case that gastronomy is in fact a fine art on par with art, literature, and music. Not that Steingarten is entirely convinced, insisting that three conditions must be met, if we are to accept this redefinition of fine dining: "the sense of taste must be put on a par with our other senses; it must be capable of the same subtle manipulation as all the others; and the entire enterprise of gastronomy must be seen to possess a meaning, an emotional and moral content." Convinced on points one and two, Steingarten confesses to uncertainty on number three. But in asking myself now where I come down on the same questions, I realize that I cannot personally read *The Passionate Epicure* as anything but a sly send-up of an utterly debased and decadent set of values—celebrating, as it does, a fat, rich, vain, arrogant, childless, loveless glutton without an earthly interest beyond the satisfactions of his own palate.

I'm open to the idea that this is just me—that I'm revealing some Anglo-American Puritanical streak that makes me ill-suited to the very highest of gastronomical heights. But it hardly matters: the *Chez Panisse Menu Cookbook* had been written in a spirit of uncritical surrender to epicurean pleasure, not least because such a spirit animated the Chez Panisse kitchen itself, in those years. Alice had written the book, after all, not as a straightforward manual to the restaurant's fine-dining cuisine but as a document of its formative, experimental phase, beginning shortly after she came onto my own family's radar as that cute little teacher down at Berkeley Montessori. She'd been living nearby, with the director of the Pacific Film Archive, already populating her locally famous dinner parties with culture heroes like Francis Ford Coppola, Jean-Luc Godard, Susan Sontag, Abbie Hoffman, and Huey Newton, leader of the Black Panthers. Then Alice got herself fired from the massive responsibility of making morning snack for me and the other toddlers by wearing see-through blouses too many days in a row. (Alice herself told me this, years later, still tickled by her own audacity.) And so she pursued her other great passion, opening Chez Panisse in 1971 and watching it bloom fast into a success. Jeremiah Tower, the dominant head chef of that period, and the author of *California Dish: What I Saw (and Cooked) at the American Culinary Revolution*, describes sous-chefs sucking nitrous in the kitchen, a prep cook named Willy Bishop painting "watercolors of guys jerking off and cum flying all over the place," and culinary frivolity like a Salvador Dalí dinner, immortalized in the *Chez Panisse Menu Cookbook*, featuring "*l'entre-plat drogué et sodomisé*," leg of lamb "drugged and sodomized" with Madeira, brandy, and tangerine juice injected through a syringe. This Bishop character claimed later to have slept with both Tower and Alice, though not at the same time. In *The United States of Arugula*, David Kamp writes that so many cocaine dealers became Chez Panisse regulars that Greil Marcus, a Chez Panisse investor and, more to the point, rock-and-roll critic, couldn't stand eating there anymore. Tower and Bishop both got hooked on blow, and Bishop graduated to a novel opium-delivery method: "You stick it up your ass," he later said to Kamp. "Just a quarter of a gram, a little ball, and you bypass the alimentary canal—you don't get nauseous, you just absorb it." Bishop lost his cooking job and his mind and later stabbed a guy in a bar, with his paring knife, on a night when he'd been planning to "go to a triple-X movie theater and stab myself. Not to kill myself, but to get attention."

Even the birth pangs of the modern Chez Panisse, acted out in this period, carry the exuberant dissolution of the midseventies: Tower, for example, quite literally seducing the 350-pound James Beard into mentioning Chez Panisse in a syndicated column. ("Getting somebody to write about you is the same as getting them to sleep with you, and I'd had a lot of practice in that," Tower writes.) When Beard dined there on the day after Christmas of 1975, Jeremiah confessed that he wasn't yet satisfied, thought of going to France.

"Jim gave me the smile he reserved for young men he held in

favor," writes Tower. "'Darling,' he said, 'keep your mouth shut about all that. You have a good thing going here, you're on the right track. Just stick with America.'"

The next morning, in what I consider the single most fabulous anecdote in my town's food history, Jeremiah claims to have visited Beard in his room at the Stanford Court Hotel, in San Francisco: "I bandaged his feet (devastated by lack of circulation), giving his devoted servant Marion Cunningham a rest from her daily chore. His robe had been left open where it fell, exposing a belly as vast as Yosemite's El Capitan, which swept down to reveal what he could have been proud to reveal were Jim not the exception to the rule that large fingers are also a measure of the family jewels. Jim did have very big hands. This was a morning ritual, exposure to which I had long since become familiar and with which I'd grown comfortable over the years I'd known him. After a little fondle, we talked about my career, about Alice." They also talked more about this idea of sticking with America, Jeremiah claims, especially California, and that's how a passing hotel-room frolic triggered the first great salvo in the creation of California cuisine, a Chez Panisse "Northern California Menu" immortalized in the *Chez Panisse Menu Cookbook*: Tomales Bay Bluepoint Oysters on Ice paired with a Schramsberg bubbly; Cream of Fresh Corn Soup, Mendocino Style, with Crayfish Butter; Big Sur Garrapata Creek Smoked Trout Steamed over California Bay Leaves, with a Mount Eden Chardonnay; Monterey Bay Prawns Sautéed with Garlic, Parsely, and Butter; Preserved California-Grown Geese from Sebastopol with a BV Private Reserve Cabernet; Vela Dry Monterey Jack Cheese from Sonoma, with a Ridge Zinfandel; Fresh Caramelized Figs.

Beautiful stuff, in a way: Tower, Beard, Dodin-Bouffant, the meteoric genius of the young Alice, forever changing our national conversation about food. But I was approaching the *Chez Panisse Menu Cookbook* in such an uncritical way, knowing nothing of its past and not yet admitting to myself that I did not have the intestinal fortitude for its implied lifestyle. So eager was I to "bond with the like-minded" that I willed our friends right on through the "Spring" menu of wild mushrooms, spring-vegetable pasta, charcoal-grilled salmon and Buckwheat Crepes with Tangerines. "Summer" came next, and then "Fall," hosted again by Rich, and including Smoked Trout Mousse with Chervil Butter, Warm Salad of Curly Endive and Artichoke Hearts, and Champagne Sauerkraut, a.k.a. Choucroute Garnie, the great Alsatian heart-stopper for which we filled a big roasting pan with four pounds of sauerkraut, a quart of duck fat, a pound of pig skin, two pounds of bacon, two suckling-pig's feet, a "prosciutto bone," a quart of chicken stock, half a bottle of Champagne, two pounds of potatoes, several suckling-pig loin chops, and a pound each of Virginia ham and garlic sausage. Baking that monstrosity whole, we set it upon the table, handed out plates, and tried hard to convince our befuddled wives that it was just a key stage in our collective education about regional French culinary variation, as if such an education mattered to anybody in the room.

Liz, in particular, found that meal so absurd that even before we got to "Winter," the writing was on the wall. We'd reentered that long, dark newborn tunnel—that snuggly and love-filled but still tough passage. The older child, about now, suffers the first grand disappointment of her life: the sibling she's wanted for a playmate turns out only to scream, cry, and dominate Mommy's love, and this turns the eldest hard toward Daddy, himself in a state of emotional deprivation and need, such that a great new bond forms and the man begins to realize that he loves fatherhood above all else. Night after night, Hannah would cry if left alone in her dark bedroom, so I would lie on her bedroom floor, right next to the crib we still had her in. She'd reach a tiny arm through the bars and wrap a tiny hand around one of my garlicky fingers. We'd doze off together, and then I'd wake up around midnight. The baby, Audrey, still owned my usual spot in the marital bed, but we'd taken over the front half of the downstairs flat by then, converting it into a pair of home offices. So I'd tiptoe out the front door and down the front steps and then back inside through the lower flat's front door, onto the extra bed next to Liz's writing desk, Mason jar for a bedpan.

Even I'd begun to falter, in commitment to all those menus, when I forced "Winter" into being, enlisting our usual crew but somehow doubling the guest list to seventeen, so that I spent more money than even I could bear. All day long, I shucked oysters until my fingers bled and I made Victoria's Champagne Sausages by hand, stuffing sheep intestines with all that pork and a whole bottle of Champagne. Together, Rich and I roasted nine whole ducks stuffed with corn bread and chanterelle mushrooms. We made duck stock from scratch; we reduced it for the sauce. Leslie made Red Onion Tarts. Clara made a Garden Lettuce Salad with Roquefort Vinaigrette. Kate made masterful Lemon Clove Cookies. And although everybody had fun, I nearly destroyed the duck sauce and I had to spend hours cleaning all the duck fat out of the oven and I began to wonder why I was so determined to make all my friends help me run a free restaurant at such great emotional and financial expense.

When I called Rich the following morning, he finally brought us to the point I could not have reached on my own. He said, "Dude, I'm really sorry. But my wife says I can't do any more dinners with you, ever. Like, not ever *ever*."

Kate, speaking through Liz herself, gently communicated

that other members of the crowd felt tired, too: "I guess maybe Kate's wondering if we could try something different next time, like an Indian-food potluck, where we all bring an Indian dish and a six-pack, and maybe pick up some naan from Aslam's Rasoi, over on Valencia."

Badly stung—I'm a social person, I care dearly about other people's opinions of me—I still wasn't man enough for random Indian potlucks, a return to my old Chicken Tikka days. ("Are you fucking kidding me? I'd rather eat glass.") So I tried to carry on alone, for a while, cooking the "Cassoulet" menu for my mother's Christmas party, and then a few other menus here and there. But by the time Audrey turned one I could no longer kid myself: I had lost my Chez Panisse faith, and it wasn't coming back.

PART THREE
What Is Cooking For?

8
The Meat Period in Every Man's Life

Anthony Lane, writing in the *New Yorker*, has wondered why so many of the best food writers are women: Alice, M. F. K., Kamman, Reichl, David. The answer, he suspects, lies in their presumed understanding "that it is enough to be a great cook, whereas men, larded with pride in their own accomplishment, invariably try to go one step too far and become great *chefs*—a grander calling, though somehow less respectable, and certainly less responsive to human need." Mea culpa, as charged, and not of mere culinary misdemeanors, like wearing a toque around the house, or demanding that my toddler daughters call me "Chef" (although Audrey once did, reading me like a book, at age three, playing for laughs, "'scuze me, Chef!"), but of the full domestic felony. Set adrift by the end of my Chez Panisse years, I'd been unable to find a cookbook that compelled me toward completionist fantasies. Without any dreams of cookbook completion, I could no longer bring myself even to tick off recipes. Soon, I'd developed the notion that, instead of torturing my wife with grand meals for peace-loving friends, I should simply commit myself to culinary woodshedding, the private study of discreet skills that a chef might someday need, even if he never planned to earn his living by the knife: bread-making, for example, with sourdough starters eternally on my person, even in the back of the car, so that I would never miss a feeding; and then knife-sharpening, for which I bought several Japanese wet stones and began studying knife-geek videos, learning to prove sharpness by dry-shaving my forearms. A guy at the Ferry Plaza Farmers Market told me about a fish distribution warehouse that would sell super-fresh product to walk-ins, if you called ahead. So I bought a book called *Rick Stein's Complete Seafood*, befriended the men down at the cavernous Ports Seafood distribution warehouse, and made a stab toward becoming a fish master—although Liz began worrying that shellfish, in particular, bothered her stomach. (Ridiculous, in my view; purely emotional female reaction to my claiming a traditionally female power in the home, the power over diet, dinner.)

But then I read, along with every other American foodie, the two obvious food-related bestsellers of that moment: *Heat: An Amateur's Adventures as Kitchen Slave, Line Cook, Pasta-Maker, and Apprentice to a Dante-Quoting Butcher in Tuscany*, by Bill Buford; and *The Omnivore's Dilemma: A Natural History of Four Meals*, by Michael Pollan. Buford chronicled a mentorship under Mario Batali, learning to cook inside Batali's restaurant kitchens, and also the fun he'd had in butchering a whole pig at home. ("One of the chicest things a chef or committed foodie can do today is pick up a whole pig from an organic farm and portion it out, cooking its defrosted chops and trotters for months to come," writes Sara Dickerman, in a seminal essay from the period, titled "Some Pig: The Development of the Piggy Confessional.") Pollan, for his part, documented hunting and killing a wild pig, and he explained that so-called commodity meat, along with factory-raised pork and poultry, emerged from such unhealthy and morally revolting circumstances that no self-respecting person could ever eat it again. Pollan also explained that holistically raised animal foods, from truly old-fashioned livestock operations, occupied a polar opposite position, clearly being the most ethically defensible and nutritious food known to mankind. Taken together, these two books laid out everything that men like me suddenly felt they had to do—the restaurant cooking, the butchery, the killing—in order to maintain perfect self-respect. So I sat up in bed one night, set down my hardcover copy of *The Omnivore's Dilemma*, and told Liz that our family was forever done eating industrial meat, and that I would like her to hand over the laptop so that I might google "grassfed beef california" and start bringing home the real bacon.

Within minutes, I'd found a local rancher, and then I ordered half a grassfed cow. That's when I got the first surprise of what I now consider the Meat Period, a standard developmental phase of the emotionally isolated male cook: Liz was all for it. It felt like nesting, made her feel warm inside. So I filled a chest freezer with a hundred pounds, vacuum-packed and labeled. A quarter of the mass came in delicious, money-shot steaks. (Yours truly: "To me, it tastes more like beef *should* taste; I can't even eat supermarket beef anymore. It totally makes me feel bloated.") Even the girls loved that stuff, and it was fun holding little Audrey in one arm, flipping meat on the grill with the other, drinking a beer and watching Audrey try to say the word *steak*. ("Want 'teak, Dada. Want 'teak.") But the next little surprise came from the ground beef comprising half my haul, and largely responsible for bringing down our total per-pound price: that's a lot of goddamn hamburgers, but Hannah turned out to be a burger fiend, and Liz loved the meat's leanness. She loved also the casual, no-big-deal feel of all those family burger nights, even if I wouldn't allow anybody to eat a burger in any manner except the Chez Panisse–approved deal with toasted levain bread, homemade aioli, grilled red onions, and arugula (I've since dropped that silliness, embracing ketchup).

Fully one quarter of my beef, however, came in oddities like crossrib roasts, top round roasts, and even tongue and other organ meats. This, in turn, led to the next scripture in the Education of the Peaceful Carnivore: *The River Cottage Meat Book*, by Hugh Fearnley-Whittingstall. The book opened with graphic slaughter-house photography and text arguing that shrink-wrapped super-market steaks, while cheap, easy, and comforting, allowed us to ignore the hard truths. Opening our eyes, by contrast, and watching that which we feared to watch, could force a man to care exactly how his meat lived and died, offering a pathway not toward shame but toward virtuous pride, when you made the right meat-buying decisions. *The River Cottage Meat Book* included a list of moral exhortation titled "My Meat Manifesto," and I had the first few in the bag. Topping the list was an order to "think about the meat that you eat," and to ask, "Is it good enough? Good enough to bring you pleasure every time you eat it?" Check. Same for encomium number two: "Think about the animals from which the meat that you eat comes." And so on, and so forth, and because *The River Cottage Meat Book* carried an epic dissertation on proper roasting technique, I'd even paid all due respect and justice to the butcher beef itself, as per instructions. But this meant discovering that all those big grassfed roasts were so lean and tough they were borderline inedible if you cooked them beyond rare, a situation that made a man look wistfully upon his dwindling steak reserves.

At this point in the Meat Period, our man wants to feel that he has climbed to significant heights. So he congratulates himself on the view back down toward those unenlightened souls still blindly devouring lethal, immoral, world-destroying garbage meat. Blocking the meaty summit, however, stands another admonition in that Meat Manifesto: "Are you adventurous with meat? Do you explore the different tastes and textures of the various cuts, particularly the cheaper cuts, and of offal?"

Thus begins the predictable Odd Bits Sub-Phase, kicked off in my own case by a visit to a neighborhood restaurant called Incanto. Chef Chris Cosentino was specializing in cooking super-gross stuff in delicious ways, so I ordered up a clear broth garnished by goose testicles and soft-shell goose eggs harvested from inside the bird's reproductive tract, a kind of Goose Fuck Soup, if you will. Then I asked to speak to the chef. I told him I was dazzled by what he was doing, and he told me that his food was not about shock value at all, nor about gross-out challenges, and that anybody who thought such foolishness was some kind of squeamish rube who didn't get it. I loved the sound of this. I loved also Cosentino's insistence that there was simply something immoral about eating only the choicest cuts from a given animal—killing all those living creatures, only to discard most of their remains.

Spooning a goose ball into my mouth, I bit until it burst and thought of a Mary Douglas book I'd read in graduate school, *Purity and Danger*. Taboo, she explains, can best be understood as a "device for protecting the distinctive categories of the universe," protecting "local consensus on how the world is organized. It shores up wavering certainty. It reduces intellectual and social disorder." By that reasoning, the contemporary American revulsion toward the consumption of animal organs and extremities reflected nothing but a fear of the ill defined, parts of the animal not clearly identified as food: "Ambiguous things can seem very threatening," Douglas writes. "Taboo confronts the ambiguous and shunts it into the category of the sacred." Offal, therefore, could be seen as a category of the profane, the filthy, but also of the sacred: we don't avoid those parts of the animal because we think they'll hurt us, or because they hold toxins, we avoid them because they have associations that scare us. Eating the heart reminds us of killing, slaughterhouses, animal sacrifice; it tells us that we are bloody in a way that we don't want to feel bloody. It also indicates that we're poor, in a way, that we don't get the good parts of the animal, that we're so desperate for protein we're stuck with the off-fall. As a fearless cook, however, I had a duty to explore all flavors and to ignore silly taboos. I could not simply rule out entire aspects of the animal: I had to face them like St. Catherine of Siena when, furious at her own revulsion for the wounds she tended in others, she sought to purify herself by drinking a bowl of pus.

I asked Cosentino for cookbook suggestions, advice on how I might pursue deeper understanding of the organs and the extremities. One thing led to another and, on Cosentino's suggestion, I got a work gig taking me to London to cook with Fergus Henderson himself—a genuine kitchen education from the Maestro of the Odd Bits, Virtuoso of the Viscera. A couple of Ambien saw me through the red-eye to London. Three cappuccinos beat back the fog at Heathrow Airport, and a London taxi took me right to the bustling eight-hundred-year-old Smithfield Meat Market. Commuters hustled every which way, tiny cars buzzed by in a hurry, horns bleated and sirens rang, and hard-hat butchers hacked at hundreds of bloody animal carcasses. Seagulls cawed in the cold gray sky, and display cases openly offered products never allowed in the door of American supermarkets: lamb's balls and gory skinless goat heads with gawking eyes. Signs advertised "Offal Brokers" and "Tripe Dressers," as if these were perfectly normal businesses. Delivery trucks roared off to the city's meat shops. Historical plaques proudly celebrated the good old days when locals buried plague victims right exactly here, in mass graves, and sold their unwanted wives at this very market, and subjected religious heretics to the archaic form of horse-assisted human butchery known as drawing and quartering.

Fergus's restaurant, named St. John for the nearby Priory of the Knights of St. John, a still-active religious order that once sent Crusader monks to slaughter Muslims, sat on an unpromising street near a random pub offering "roasted ox kidney with mash and mustard sauce." Crowds of off-duty butchers, wearing white coveralls drenched in bright red animal blood, from their graveyard shifts, smoked cigarettes and devoured eggs at sidewalk tables. A wire fence surrounded the installation site of a new Urilift, a public urinal meant to rise hydraulically from the sidewalk every night at 10 P.M., when everyone stumbled drunk from the pubs. (Apparently it would vanish again at 4 A.M., every morning.)

I'd seen pictures of the old St. John building, gray and black and white, so I recognized it immediately. But the sense of disorientation began the moment I scanned a menu pinned up outside: plain white paper, black type, and a list of unfamiliar dishes presented without explanation, as if they were just the ancient standards of some long-established culture. Pigeon & Swede; Stinking Bishop & Potatoes; Roast Middlewhite; Cockles, Bacon & Laverbread; Roast Bone Marrow & Parsley Salad; Tripe, Carrots & Bacon; Smoked Eel, Bacon & Mash. And sure, a few less challenging foods, but even they carried this unusual style: Roast Beef, Turnips & Aioli; Salsify, Watercress & Poached Eggs; Skate & Monk's Beard. The disorientation deepened when I sought to enter and yet could not decide if I should use the unmarked door to the right or the car-sized tunnel to the left, leading toward double glass doors. Choosing the latter, I passed through a second set of double glass doors into an equally curious industrial space with non-parallel walls painted stark white, black metal stairs leading both up and down from odd corners of the room, absolutely no art anywhere, and a chest-height metal bar, with a bartender on an elevated platform, so that I felt as if I'd shrunk to child size, straining upward to catch the bartender's attention. When I failed, I used my cell phone to call Fergus's media-relations person, with whom I'd arranged the whole trip, securing even agreement that I'd learn to cook from Fergus himself, right in the St. John kitchen.

"You say you've come to the restaurant?" she said now, as if surprised.

"As promised, right?"

"Okay. *Right*."

"But you knew that."

"Yep, yep. Right! Okay! So, let me see if I can find Fergus."

Ten minutes later, he appeared at my shoulder: graying, buzz-cut blond hair; round and ruddy-red face a little blank due to his Parkinson's disease. Crushingly hip black plastic eyeglasses magnified Fergus's pale blue eyes, and his blue canvas smock—over a crumpled white button-down shirt—made him look like an avant-garde midcentury sculptor. He'd had major brain surgery a few years earlier, apparently controlling his Parkinson's symptoms so that he didn't tremble like Muhammad Ali. But when it came time to express himself to me, Fergus's head and left arm snapped backward and to the left, as if grabbing at words hidden behind his left shoulder. Hurling them forward again, he spoke in a curiously old-fashioned mumble, as if he'd stepped out of *The Canterbury Tales* to ask if I'd like a "mumble-mumble."

"Hmm?"

"Fernet mumble?"

"I'm afraid I don't . . ."

Fergus raised one finger and both eyebrows, like a circus performer pantomiming Not to Worry, All Shall Be Revealed. "A miracle," he said. With a wave of the hand, he had that towering bartender pour two shots of Fernet Branca, an 80 proof Italian herbal liqueur, jet black in the glass.

I was already in a vertiginous blur of half-comatose, half-speedy nausea, and I wondered aloud if I could really risk a cocktail just then, but Fergus said, "Cures all known ailments. Might sort you out."

So I drank my shot and felt a kind of calm sweeping over me. Then Fergus said, "Well, any interest in seeing the kitchen?"

"Ah . . . well, of course. Right?"

"Righty ho. So, let's go."

Crossing the white St. John dining room, Fergus entered the kitchen but stayed carefully out of the way of the men doing the actual cooking. In one corner of that small, busy room—a room in which I imagined Fergus and I would soon dive into chopping, cutting, and cooking together—I saw hotel pans piled with beef hearts bigger than cantaloupes. A veteran chef from another restaurant, working without pay to get his ticket punched, set each heart on a cutting board, trimmed away the hard white fat and gristle, sliced apart the heart chambers, cut off the big gaping veins and arteries, and then cut the dark red heart meat into slices thin enough for char-grilling. I paid special attention, so that I'd be a quick study when it came to be my turn; same with another outside chef, also volunteering, working through a box of lamb kidneys. One by one, I noted, he set those little red organs on the counter, cut out these weird white lobes inside—*I can do that*, I thought—and moved the kidneys to another tray, where he'd toss them with a spicy dry rub. A heavily tattooed deliveryman arrived carrying a white plastic crate with an aged side of beef that also happened to be dripping blood all over the restaurant floor and down the deliveryman's ornately decorated forearms (not aged enough, apparently). Cursing in rage, the deliveryman wiped himself off, left the room, and returned with a crate full of skinless rabbits looking more like headless, footless greyhounds that had been killed mid-run, legs extended. Another white plastic case carried pigeons individually wrapped in plastic—little dark lumps the size of your fist.

A third cook—on the payroll, this one—chopped up what Fergus told me were "chitterlings, pigs' poop pipes," to be fried in duck fat and served with radishes. A fourth chef, slicing a big deer's liver, paused to show us where a bullet had plowed through, leaving an ugly hole. Then Fergus cracked open the heavy door of St. John's walk-in refrigerator, and I ducked as I trailed him inside, entering a cold low-ceilinged space where packed shelves carried chickens still attached to their own heads and feet, a complete leg of a lamb, looking very much like a leg, and massive piles of marrow bones. Figuring I'd have to run in here chasing some ingredient or other, I made mental notes of the pork livers wrapped in muslin cloth just like my own at home—dried in a mixed cure of salt and sugar. I took notice of the big sheets of pig skin, too, waiting to be cut up and cooked either as cracklings or as a way to add gelatin—and thus body—to various soups, stocks, and braises. A big bucket brimmed with suckling pigs: pretty pink-skinned babies, still looking young and happy, as if they'd been napping in the sun when the power went out.

Back in the dining room, we took a table and talked for a while, and then Fergus ordered us a round of Champagne and several dishes for lunch, which I considered unnecessary, but a fine way to warm up toward our cooking sessions. The St. John dining room had begun to fill, and Fergus raised his glass and we both drank.

Then he said, "So, what brings you . . . to London?"

"What?"

"London. All that way, California. Anything particular? Friends? Family?"

"They didn't tell you?"

"Me?"

"I've come to write an article. About you."

"Oh, right."

"I hope that's okay."

"Of course! But that's all? That's why you've come?"

"No other business."

Fergus's eyes widened. "Right." He fell into thought. Then he said, in a gentle and considerate way, "Well, don't fret. We'll make sure you get everything you need, and that you have a good time. What do you need, anyway?"

I mentioned that I'd hoped we might cook together. Before he answered, we both looked down at a plate of duck hearts, little brown marbles atop a soft white mound of celeriac purée. Ox heart arrived next, thin sheets of that grilled meat, with a strongly flavored salad. Yet another plate held four upright marrow bones, each about three inches tall. These were slender veal leg bones— "like a lady's ankle," as Fergus described them, explaining that adult beef bones would look more like they'd come from rugby players. And then, at last, those chitterlings, the pig's poop pipes, "though they've been brined quite far away from all that," Fergus insisted, as if this could put me at ease.

Fergus emptied his Champagne glass, so I did the same, noticing that it was now only 11:30 A.M. Then the waiter set down a bottle of Burgundy and filled glasses for us both.

"Well, stab a heart," Fergus said.

I found the marrow dish especially intoxicating—picking up a roasted bone, digging a knife into the marrow hole, scooping out the whitish-gray muck and then spreading it on toasted bread. Coarse gray sea salt lay in a pile on the plate, and the idea was to grab a pinch, sprinkle it atop the marrow on your bread, do the same with some of that parsley, and enjoy. I tried the ox heart next, and positively loved the dense, intense muscle fiber. So I asked Fergus the difference between this and pig heart.

"Right," he said. "Well, by nature *being* hearts, hearts are the heart of the beast . . . ox heart really expresses . . . *ox.*"

He paused, as if worried that this sounded flip, or like a game he was playing with me. "Little duck hearts express . . . ducks, going bubumpbubumpbumpbubump. It's an extraordinary expression of the beast they come from . . ."

He paused again, deep in thought. Then he finished the first glass of wine and poured another and topped off my own glass and said, "I like organs. They look like themselves."

"Like kidneys," I offered, thinking you'd certainly never mistake one for a rib eye.

"Kidneys," Fergus said, visibly brightening. "There's a magical *squeak*, when you bite them . . . and then a . . . *give.*"

Fergus spoke in curious stops and starts, like an experimental jazz drummer so contrapuntal you couldn't tap your foot. He told me about spleen, too: "It's wonderful, it swells in . . ."

"It swells in your mouth?"

"In love. It swells in *love*, which can be seen as a good thing or a bad thing, depending . . ." Pause. "That's the brilliant thing about offal. You find these textures you don't find in anything else. A *squeak* . . ."

Pause.

". . . andthena*giiivve* . . ."

Pause.

"We devil the kidneys . . . usually," he said. "In well-seasoned flour . . . It's my birthday breakfast. It sets you up very *very* well. And I believe it's that *squeak* that acts as a sort of . . . *Cupid* to me. Like brains, it's a textural experience."

"Brains, right. Okay, so why don't we talk about brains. What culinary potential do you see bound up in a brain?"

"Well, we poach them very gently, separate the lobes, and then . . . we bread and fry them. You get this *crunch* and then this rich, creamy give and . . . *gna!*"

"Gna?" It appeared to be a moan of delight.

"Maybe a green sauce, cornichons, capers . . . it's sort of the *Gna!* Theory of Brains, so . . . that you have a couple of bites and it's *so* delicious and it's so rich and you sort of . . . *gna!* In fact, there's some . . ."

Long pause, twitching.

". . . story . . ."

Even longer pause, and even more twitching.

"Someone said, oh, I can't remember, '. . . all those memories!'"

"In a brain?"

"Ah!" He smiled. "There we go. But look, there's one thing . . . sometimes it's sort of entertainment for City boys in here. 'Who's going to eat the most scary thing on the menu!' And that gives you the wrong . . . Nothing's scary. It's all delicious."

Flying home, back to Liz and the girls, I felt that he was right: everything I'd eaten, in both of his restaurants, was indeed delicious. I even tried to emulate him, for a little while. Certain ingredients made that easy: my gigantic grassfed cow's heart, for example, looked and tasted much like the ox heart at St. John, and I loved eating it. To this day, it's a favorite dish of mine. But soon I felt a very different thought overtaking me, especially when I looked through my livers and my kidneys from those grown-up cows and pigs, in my freezer: Fergus used none of these things. He cooked all the parts of animals, yes, but he didn't cook all the parts of any one animal. Duck hearts, sure, but not chicken hearts; ox hearts, but only from a single farm in Ireland; adult pig hearts, never, although sometimes the heart of a suckling pig; marrow bones, indeed, but only from calves, and therefore never from the same adult cattle providing the hearts or the big sides of beef, and therefore also imported from Denmark, given that England no longer had much of a veal industry at all. And so on: calf liver, but not cow liver; lamb's brains, but not pig's brains. Fergus was indeed masterful with unusual proteins, but his real gift—the quiet, unsung source of his power, I decided—lay rather in the clarity with which he'd realized his own idiosyncratic vision. Organs and extremities contributed to that vision, but not as ends in themselves. They were ingredients, rather, props in the generation of an alternate reality, a parallel universe in which British history had taken a slightly different turn about a century back, arriving at a slightly different present tense in which small English farms coexisted with the monstrous modern London, creek and hedgerow still teemed with squirrels to braise and eels to bake. Which was nice and everything, but applicable to Northern California only as an abstract example, not a concrete map for how to eat, or to feed one's family.

9
My Kung Fu Is Not Strong

Back before we got married, Liz and I presented her sister, Debbie, with a birthday present of Thomas Keller's *The French Laundry Cookbook*. Neither Keller's name nor his three-Michelin-star restaurant meant a thing to me at the time. Judy suggested the present; Liz purchased it; I paid little attention; and I knew scarcely more about Keller when Jon, the liquor exec from the Menu Period, gave me Keller's second cookbook as a gift. Named for the casual bistro Keller had opened just down the road from the French Laundry, *Bouchon* struck me initially as a cookbook not to use but to set on the coffee table, telling guests that you'd been to the mountaintop. (An ancient genre, according to Jane Kramer, who reports seeing sixteenth-century versions, at the home of the French-cookbook historians Mary and Philip Hyman, of what the Hymans called the "here's what's happening at the table where you'll never be allowed to sit" cookbooks.) I felt a little stunned, too, by Keller's utter lack of even the slightest nod toward Chez Panisse in *Bouchon*. No mention of Alice, nor of the hallowed California principles of seasonality, locality, and sustainability. I found myself thinking, in a grouchy mood, *Who do you think you are!? Don't you know Queen Alice reigns in these parts?* Flipping through *The French Laundry*, as I did at Debbie's house one evening, only worsened my outrage: in a reference to a French chef working in Washington, D.C., in the late 1970s, Keller described him as the first chef in America to seek out fine produce from local farmers. It was like Keller imagined himself working not in the California that Alice built—not in a bountiful landscape full of boutique bakers and specialty farmers eager to sell him great ingredients—but in some timeless, placeless haute-cuisine tradition reaching back through his own mentor, Roland Henin (currently the head chef of the Yosemite National Park concessions, in a truly weird tangling of destinies), to every great French chef who had ever lived.

Now, however, I found myself a little intrigued: Keller was almost the perfect anti-Alice, the ideal post-Fergus. If Alice had embodied the maternal home-cooking lineage through which I'd gotten started, and if Fergus dominated a more experimental approach for which I simply did not have either the adventurous palate or the catholic audience, perhaps I could see Keller as the embodiment of the great chef-driven lineage running directly from Temples of Gastronomy like Paris's Taillevent to the New York restaurants of Alain Ducasse and Daniel Boulud, and straight on up to the French Laundry. Perhaps I could see Keller, in other words, as my link to an unassailably classic tradition, the study of which might qualify as unassailably meaningful. As for Bouchon itself, it did feel a bit like Manhattan's Balthazar or Pastis, a perfect Hollywood-worthy replica of a Lyon bistro, plopped into a different world—perhaps even more so in that Bouchon's world was Keller's hometown, the sleepy agricultural village of Yountville. And the food: Blanquette de Veau; Poule au Pot; Steak Frites; Quiche Lorraine; bistro classics presented in rigorous homage to an urban French restaurant form; the Napa Valley, a coincidental backdrop.

Soon, however, I found myself seduced by the photographs in

Bouchon, the restaurant elegance of the food and the casual professionalism of this Keller guy and his gorgeous girlfriend, shown relaxing over red wine and mussels, within Keller's own place of business. Not one Chez Panisse cookbook, I realized, offered a single photograph of the restaurant, a chef, or even a plated Chez Panisse meal. Not one, in nine books. Everything about their conception seemed to encourage one's own imagination. Meditating on such images now, in *Bouchon*, I sought out and found similar ones in *The French Laundry*, over at Debbie's house—slightly out of focus, shot from eye level in a blur, as if to simulate being in the French Laundry kitchen, during service. The whole idea was to fuel the consumer's love affair with restaurants and professional chefs, and with remarkable speed those photographs ushered me toward what Nicholas Lemann has called toque envy: hoping that I might become "practically indistinguishable from a real chef, except that—really just a tiny difference—you would be cooking at home instead of at a restaurant." Lemann pins me like a lepidopterist's butterfly when he writes that "chef has become, to a certain type of urban adult, what astronaut is to a seven-year-old boy—the standard fantasy occupation." *Bouchon* didn't just offer photographs, either; it offered magically precise instructions for the simplest of salads, explaining every nuance of every step and technique required to get bistro-level results. I began to think that, even if we weren't going to have huge dinner parties anymore, perhaps Liz would let me try to impress her parents, the greatest restaurant-goers I knew. They'd gotten me started in the first place, I'd come a long way, they'd actually been to Bouchon, and yet I hadn't cooked for them once, ever.

Doug and Judy had moved to California by this point: sold their Massachusetts home, rented a San Francisco pied-à-terre, and bought a golf-resort condo in the Napa Valley. We'd since eaten Judy's great cooking at both of these places—San Francisco and Napa—and Doug had treated us all to many restaurant meals. So I suggested hosting them.

Liz agreed, several weeks passed, and nothing happened.

I suggested it again.

Liz agreed, and several more weeks passed, and nothing happened.

So I asked: Baby, what gives? They don't want to eat with us? They don't believe I can cook?

Liz claimed to have no idea what I was talking about.

"Well, just tell me what exactly happens when you invite them."

"I don't," she said.

"What do you mean?"

"I don't really want my parents here for dinner."

"I ask you to invite them, and you just don't?"

"I'd be too tense."

"About what, the messy kitchen?"

"Maybe."

Or the house. "It's the fucking house, isn't it?"

Playing with fire, now: Liz had been freaking out about living space, all four of us crammed into 750 square feet, and she'd gotten this idea that we should convert her downstairs office into a new parental bedroom, getting us a little nighttime privacy and allowing each of our daughters to have a separate room. My own office could then become Liz's office, and I could move my desk maybe into the basement, over between the two water heaters, by the gas furnace. She had a point; we did have a tiny place, and we did have growing children, and it really was stupid having our single biggest room occupied only by Liz's tiny desk and laptop. New challenges looming, in other words; family needs going in new directions, well beyond that old "somebody cooks dinner while somebody changes the diapers" formulation. But I told Liz that, piss-filled Mason jars notwithstanding (she'd found a half-full one next to her computer keyboard, remnant of the sleep I was still getting in her office), we still had a palace by the standards of 99.9 percent of humanity. Liz replied that A) she wasn't interested in 99.9 percent of humanity, and B) she didn't think hoping for a grand total of 1,250 square feet to raise a family in made her a spoiled bitch. I pointed out that I would never, ever call her such a thing, and that I was pretty sure that Buddhism (or Hinduism, I didn't know which) taught that all suffering came from desire, and that Liz could liberate *me* from all *my* suffering by letting go of *her* desire for another room. Liz then demonstrated, convincingly, that we spent more on wine and groceries every month than on our mortgage, and that I might therefore want to hold fire on desire-equals-suffering.

Liz doesn't like a fight. She's strong. She's proud. But she's a peacemaker, and she cares for me the best she can, so she found a compromise, threw me a bone: she got her mother to let me cook dinner at the Napa place. *Bouchon*'s Roast Chicken with Summer Squash and Tomatoes (*Poulet Rôti aux Courgettes et Tomates Persillées*), sounded easy enough, and it really wasn't a bad choice, but I didn't read the recipe until midday of the dinner in question, well after buying all the ingredients. Sitting in Judy's immaculate white Napa kitchen, with only six hours to go, I noticed that right there, within the ingredients list, Keller called not just for "two chickens," but for "two 2¼ to 2½ pound chickens, brined for 6 hours as directed on page 192 and drained." Everything still could've turned out fine if I'd recognized that—even in the narrowest definition of my own self-interest—the next little step in my private pursuit of technical improvement was far less important than delivering a safe, simple, no-fuss family meal, on time and with minimal domestic disruption. In other words, I could've chosen not to brine, but then I wouldn't have learned the primary restaurant-chef lesson I thought Keller was offering to teach here, so I flipped to page 192 and saw not only crystal-clear instructions for immersing the birds in the brine, but a note that, for the brine itself, I'd have to turn to page 325, where the masterful brine recipe began, disappointingly, as follows: "It is a good idea to make this brine a day ahead and refrigerate it. Don't add meat to warm brine and don't leave it in brine longer than the specified time or it may become too salty."

I hadn't even begun, and I was two days behind. But I was also stunned by how much this *Bouchon* book had to teach, far more than any Chez Panisse book even attempted. And so, badly wanting to be man enough for *Bouchon*, I rummaged around in poor Judy's beloved cabinets until I found a large pot to hold a gallon of water, a cup of salt, a dollop of honey, a dozen bay leaves, a half cup of garlic cloves, two tablespoons of black peppercorns, a few rosemary sprigs and a bunch of thyme, and some grated lemon zest. Then I waited anxiously while this took twenty minutes to boil, and only after it boiled did I wonder how the hell I was going to chill it fast enough to get the birds in. The only solution I could see at the time was to pull everything out of Judy's well-stocked freezer—party ice, frozen peas, Ben & Jerry's, frozen waffles—and shove them into Ziploc bags dug from a drawer and then immerse all those bags in the chicken brine, to cool it down. I still have no idea why I thought that was acceptable behavior, without permission, in my mother-in-law's kitchen, but I did. Nor did I see a problem with clearing stuff from Judy's fridge to make room for the big brining pot, once I'd added the chickens. So I did that, too, and then I up and left the house for several hours, off to the golf-resort spa—Jacuzzi, steam, magazine in the sunshine, thinking I'd pull together dinner at the last minute. When I returned at four thirty, still with a couple of hours before dinner, Doug and Judy were entertaining three surprise visitors: the adult daughter of a dearly missed Massachusetts couple, this daughter's husband, and their baby. Judy felt awful that she'd double-booked her afternoon, arranging to play golf with some new California acquaintances. But Liz reassured her mother that we'd look after the Massachusetts couple, and that we could all have dinner together later. Judy left; and I went to look at the chicken, finding a surprise: Judy had taken her frozen goods out of my brine pot and put them all back in her freezer, so as not to ruin them. She'd also put my brining chickens out on the back porch in the ninety-degree sunshine, to make room for her milk, eggs, and butter to go back into the refrigerator. A quiet desperation overtook me. Feeling punked, humiliated, but still focused on triumph, I took the milk, eggs, and butter back *out* of Judy's fridge, and put the chicken back *in* Judy's fridge, and made a mess chopping all the herbs and vegetables for the zucchini and tomato sides. Then, sometime around five o'clock, I felt seized by the need to leave that mess in place and go buy some running shoes.

I didn't even run, back then.

With dinner due on the table at seven o'clock sharp, to allow the Massachusetts couple time for the drive home to San Francisco, I put Liz in the station wagon and drove twenty minutes away to buy shoes that brought me no satisfaction, and for reasons that remain to this day utterly mysterious.

Then we drove back, I pulled the chickens out of the brine, I dumped out the brine, and I discovered that I was now supposed to truss the chickens, yet another move I'd never attempted, but would not consider forgoing. I went through twenty feet of string trying to follow the *Bouchon* directions, and once I'd gotten it I asked Liz to preheat the oven and put in the birds while I got banging on those vegetables. At ten minutes before seven, Judy came back and set the table frantically and asked how long until the chickens would be done (half an hour, minimum) and quietly started cleaning up the mess I'd created. The other couple, meanwhile, grew visibly anxious to escape.

Hannah, by that point, had completely turned her back on all food except hot dogs, macaroni-and-cheese, and chocolate croissants. So I let Liz whip together a kid dinner while we waited for the chicken. When the timer finally sounded, I opened the oven door, and the birds sat there cold and raw. The oven was not on.

I wanted to leave. I wanted simply to walk out the front door and never come back. I told myself this was everybody's fault but my own.

"Time to order pizza," I said to Liz.

The woman from Massachusetts said to a mortified Judy, "Hey, you know, it's really okay. You don't have to feed us. We should probably just head on back to the city."

"No, no!" Judy said. "Don't go anywhere! I'll get steaks! Don't leave!" She grabbed her keys and purse and bolted out the door. Just for the hell of it, I turned on the oven, put the birds in, and took a long solo walk in the cul-de-sac night. I saw a mother deer and a fawn, silhouetted against the blue-black Napa sky, out on the golf course. Liz put the girls to sleep while I was gone, and I returned so ashamed of myself I couldn't make eye contact with our famished and frantic guests, who wished only to be liberated from this family psychodrama. Then we all heard Judy's car honking as she sped up the block, sending out a sonic signal that help was on the way: *Beep! Beep!* She screeched into the garage, honked yet again, jumped out of the Infiniti, and ran inside yelling,

"Steaks! I've got steaks!" Firing up a skillet, she slapped them in there, seared both sides, and set the steaks on the table, somewhere around 8:30 P.M. I set my cooked chickens right alongside, so that we could all eat in silence.

The next morning, Liz informed me that I was forever banned from cooking anything—ever again—at the Napa place. This stung far worse even than the menu crowd's collapse, and I do believe it triggered in me a deeply helpful upwelling of confusion, a sense that I was still missing some critical lesson. But I responded in the short term by doubling down, certain that my salvation lay only in greater mastery. So I began reading every *Bouchon* recipe, beginning to end, a week in advance, to avoid nasty surprises. Then I'd lay out a plan of action, as with Keller's Beef Bourguignon recipe: days for the beef stock; bottle of red wine reduced to a glaze with mountains of aromatic herbs and vegetables, to provide the base into which all that stock (and still more herbs and vegetables) would then go, for the braising liquid; covering this braising medium with cheesecloth before laying down the browned meat, so the browned meat could later be removed without odd overcooked bits of vegetable. Saturday morning, the day of the dinner, went toward shopping for Keller's grand *Bouchon* shellfish platter, as my first course: giant pot of court bouillon simmering on the stove; said court bouillon used for cooking Dungeness crab, shrimp, clams. Oysters on the half-shell, mussels opened with a little steam. ("Honey," I said, exasperated, "please don't pull this bullshit *again*. There's no way my shellfish is going to make you sick. Those crabs were trying to kill me five minutes ago.") Part of being a pro chef, I figured, involved being one's own sommelier; as a result, my drinking scene spiraled toward the dangerous fantasy that wine isn't really booze, it's a form of high culture, even art. Getting plastered on wine, according to this reasoning, has less in common with, say, getting plastered than it does with evenings at the opera. We'd already fed hot dogs to the kids, and they were happily amusing themselves, so I set out all that seafood and six bottles of wine with only Amy and Martin for guests. I told them we had a rare opportunity for a comparison tasting of non-malolactic Chardonnays from the Sonoma Coast against value-priced Chablis, and this made it almost impossible for them not to get stuffed, drunk, and drawn into our latest little domestic tension.

To wit: I'd suggested building that interior stair myself, to solve our space problems; Liz, as she repeated for Martin and Amy, wanted to say, "Go for it, baby, rip down the interior chimney and tear up our house for six months, make a hash of the stairs and then demolish them in a fit of perfectionist pique and redo them three times until you're satisfied, it's all good, the girls and I want to live right through it all and stand by our man," but she ached for us to be one of those normal middle-class couples who got to hire contractors and have jobs done quickly and correctly. Amy agreed with Liz's reassertion that this *still* did not make her a spoiled bitch. I told everyone the whole subject (of the stair, not Liz's hypothetical spoiled bitchiness) was moot until we knew exactly where to put a new staircase in the first place, and then baleful screaming erupted from down the hall, sounding like the younger of Amy's two daughters. Amy sprinted in her stiletto heels into the girls' room, and somehow generated a much bigger crash and then a loud, strange, anguished cry of her own. The rest of us ran to find Amy on the floor, eyes dilating, holding one of her wrists limp in the other hand. Hannah and Amy's little girls, it turned out, had together discovered the totally hilarious game of spraying Hannah's hair detangler—silicone lubricant, in mist form—all over the wood floor, to make it smell pretty. Thus, the little slam and cry, when Amy's daughter had slipped and fallen; and likewise thus, Amy, upon rounding the bend to console her just-fallen youngest, finding herself horizontally airborne, the side of her head impacting in advance of her body. With a dark bruise already clouding her pretty cheekbone, Amy trembled and held that swelling wrist and looked me in the eye and said she was fine—that she really didn't want to miss that braised beef.

Being human, I loved this; I felt a ferocious excitement at what Keller was bringing me. *This food is so goddamned good that even after cracking her head on the floor, my guest wants more.* But I suspected it wasn't just the food; I suspected it was also Amy's intuition about how desperately I wanted everybody to applaud my creations.

I'd only just ladled a serving into each bowl when Amy confessed that her arm really was beginning to hurt.

"Do you think I might have broken it?" she asked.

"Honey, you did not break your arm," said Martin.

Looking at the wrist in question, I did see a visible bump forming fast, along one of the bones. So I faced a conundrum: lying about my true diagnosis, to make sure everybody experienced my culinary brilliance and then praised it effusively before Amy's arm ruined the night, or putting the meal aside and focusing on a friend. (As Brillat-Savarin would have it, "To invite people to dine with us is to make ourselves responsible for their well-being for as long as they are under our roofs.")

Speaking directly to me now, Amy said, "Dan, do you think I broke my arm?"

I looked at Martin, afraid to undermine my buddy.

He said, "Ames, come on! It's not broken. Let's eat!"

Amy appeared quite worried, holding that limp wrist.

I asked her to move the hand up and down, and she said that she could not.

"Okay, so here's the truth," I said. "I'm no doctor, but that's a broken arm. It would totally make sense to find an ER."

The next morning, we learned that Amy had not only broken her arm, she'd sustained a serious concussion. A few weeks later, suddenly slurring words and losing her balance, she had a new CAT scan revealing unresolved bleeding on her brain. Amy's fine now, but I still felt awful about this when Liz finally made her own trip to the emergency room. She'd invited some architect friends to dinner, looking for advice on placement of the stairs, and although I'd planned my simplest menu in months, I did put out a full *Bouchon* seafood platter, as a main course. Thus, the fateful question, from these putative friends: "So, how do you guys see remodeling the house, long-term?"

"We don't," I said. And then, catching the look on Liz's face, "I'm telling you, honey, the seafood is fresh." (Which of course it was; my fish guys were heroes, beyond reproach.)

"That's ridiculous, sweetheart. Of course we see remodeling, in the long term."

"No we don't," I replied. "Grab some crab."

She hesitated, stared at the claws groping off the dish. "How can you say that we *never* want to remodel anything, for the rest of our lives?"

"Crab."

She glared at me, grabbed some.

"More. Go on, more crab. And I'm not saying *never*. I'm saying it's not on the horizon, so why discuss it? Go on, crack the shell."

So she did.

"Pull out the meat, with a fork."

"Honey, I know how to eat crab."

Putative friend: "I'll actually have some crab, if that's okay. I love crab."

"The architect loves crab."

"And by the way, you guys, a total remodel doesn't have to be on the horizon at all. We just always encourage clients to sketch out a vision of everything they might ever want to do to a house, as a way of making sure each little project along the way fits into a bigger scheme, so you don't regret anything. We could easily draw that up for you."

"That might be great," Liz said, once again glaring at me, as I passed her the seafood platter. "How long would it take?"

"Few weeks, probably. We're not too busy."

They left, later that night, with a verbal contract to write up this so-called Master Plan. Liz told me that she really, really did not feel good. I dismissed the complaint yet again, and we fell asleep. Then I woke up alone, in our shared bed, wondering where Liz had gone. I heard my beloved's voice, somewhere else in the flat, wailing about half my too-short name—"Daa . . ."—before stopping with a distinctive thump much like Amy's body had made in hitting the floor.

So I leapt out of bed—truly spooked, sprinting naked down the hall, not funny in the moment—and I found the mother of my two young daughters facedown in a pool of beige-colored puke, directly in front of the diarrhea-filled toilet, having just blown crab, mussels, and homemade pear ice cream out both ends and then collapsed off the toilet and smacked face-first onto the floor.

"Liz," I said. "Wake up, baby."

Nothing.

"Come on, baby. Wake up."

I'd seen a few spooky things, in all those Labor and Delivery wards, but this was different. She wasn't moving, her dark brown eyes had rolled back in her head, and I couldn't get a pulse, couldn't see breathing. So I turned her over and she flopped to her back like a dead fish, hands slapping the floor. Still nothing, so I began to panic. I slapped her pretty pukey face but she didn't wake up. I grabbed underneath her arms and hoisted her to standing, hoping to hell our two young daughters didn't wake up and see me bouncing their unconscious mommy up and down. But Mommy was absolutely blank and limp and not breathing, so I laid her down again and tried to remember CPR, and I was pressing on her chest and blowing into her mouth and beginning to cry because I was thinking about two sweet little girls and how they really *need* their mommy and how I'm not man enough for single fatherhood but that I'll never remarry because I'll always love Liz and I'll devote myself to a life of selfless suffering to give the girls a great start in the world.

Then I called 911 and told the operator my wife was dying.

Two minutes, tops—they must've been in the neighborhood—four jackbooted EMTs marched up the front stairs and pounded on the door and I was naked and let them in and Liz woke up.

"Hey, honey," she said, all normal. "Why am I in the bathroom?"

The EMTs called it a vasovagal syncope—a.k.a fainting—and they told me it's perfectly natural, maybe some GI distress, drops the pulse and breathing so an untrained (read "clueless") civilian might not detect much. I told them all about my ordeal anyway, because I was proud of my CPR and I wanted a little validation that it was really cool and that maybe I'd saved her life, but the EMTs looked at each other like *Can you believe this guy?* I could have done nothing, they said, and Liz would have regained consciousness at precisely the same moment. As to the cause, they wouldn't guess, but Liz blamed the shellfish, deciding she must be allergic, and in the moment I really did think, in a fleeting sort of way, *She's making it up. Typical female resistance to the male zest for life; classic attempt to castrate, emasculate, control. She's already sworn off pigeon and pig liver, and now shellfish? What's next, fucking lettuce?*

But then those EMTs loaded Liz into their ambulance and took her to the hospital for observation. The girls slept through the whole nightmare, and I lay awake in my empty marital bed, once again picturing my sweetheart in a hospital gown. By the time she got home, via taxicab, I'd begun muttering, *My Kung Fu is not strong. My Kung Fu is not strong. I must go into the mountains, to meditate.* When I finally woke up the next morning, and looked at my sleeping wife, and thought about my sleeping daughters across the hall, I realized that I could no longer kid myself about feeding the family, or putting food on the table. Even I now saw that I'd been up to something far more complicated, and self-referential, and that I might soon have to stop.

10
On Cooking and Carpentry

Every morning, when I was in high school, I'd eat Raisin Bran while looking out the window at a sidewalk where a broad-shouldered man often walked by, on his way to work. David Goines, as a longtime boyfriend to Alice Waters, and the graphic designer behind logos for Chez Panisse and many of Berkeley's other marquee businesses, was like our very own Betsy Ross. And his personal style suggested that he and my dad were auditioning for different roles in the same Hollywood western. They both wore bushy mustaches and faded Levi's, but my dad's pointy cowboy boots and snap-button shirts placed him with the ranch hands—standard attire, in those days, for left-wing social-justice lawyers like Dad, fighting the good fight—while Goines's denim work shirt, silk vest, and comfortable leather shoes pegged him for the highly principled newspaper printer in the small western town. But the ranch hands and the printer, in this particular movie, fought on different sides of the battle over the frontier's future. Dad had grown up Irish Catholic in 1950s Los Angeles: altar boy, Eagle Scout, fraternity brother, and navy lieutenant. He was already a UC Berkeley law student dating my sorority-sister mom by the time he volunteered for civil rights work, back in Georgia, in the early sixties: politically liberal, in other words, but socially conservative, starting a family.

David Goines and Alice Waters, on the other hand, were both still undergraduates in 1964, when Dad returned from Georgia. So Dad was already a third-year law student when Goines became locally famous as one of the original student radicals surrounding a cop car and kicking off the Free Speech Movement. In a similar generational hairsplitter, Alice opened Chez Panisse during the very same week in August of 1971 when the Black Panthers buried George Jackson, a member who'd murdered three guards while trying tried to break out of San Quentin Federal Penitentiary. Kamp, in *The United States of Arugula*, has pointed out that these two events marked a fork in the road for the Berkeley political revolution, with my father's radical strain fading out while the gourmet-hedonistic movement caught wind. A lawyer friend of my father's, Fay Stender, had been Jackson's attorney in the past, even helping him write a bestselling prison memoir called *Soledad Brother*. Shortly after George Jackson died, Huey Newton himself invited Dad to his Oakland penthouse, asking Dad to represent one of Jackson's breakout accomplices, a man named Johnny Spain. Afraid of getting used, and doubtless thinking of his two little kids, Dad said he'd only take the job with fifty grand up front. That didn't work out, and Dad often reminded himself it was just as well by telling us how the Black Guerrilla Family broke into Stender's home and shot her in bed, leaving her paralyzed; she killed herself in Hong Kong in 1980.

So, while Dad backed away from criminal clients to make a safer living, Willy Bishop's heroin and Jeremiah Tower's cocaine at Chez Panisse represented everything decadent about the direction his town was trending. When that trend made its curious right turn toward bourgeois Baby Boomer complacency, and epicureanism—Chez Panisse the social epicenter of Berkeley, the place to be and be seen in the Court of Queen Alice—my father simply wanted no part.

Throughout my Chez Panisse cooking years, and especially when I mentioned Alice to my father, I'd felt this quiet little discomfort at the table, as if I were allying myself with the wrong faction in our hometown's culture wars. I felt that discomfort again when I learned that a friend of my sister's, a kind, lovely woman named Caroline, happened to work in Alice's office, running Alice's philanthropic Chez Panisse Foundation. Calling me up one day, out of the blue, Caroline said she'd heard about my cookbook-bingeing and wondered if I'd help Alice write a speech. The timing could've been better—back when I was cooking from Alice's books, for example—but it could've been worse. I felt badly frustrated by my attempts at making Keller into my final Kitchen God, the man to bring me into confident mastery; and I needed the work, not least because those architects, the putative friends tasked with telling us where to put an interior staircase, had delivered a Master Plan with the marvelous news that we could meet all our space needs, forever and ever, if we just gutted our two downstairs offices and transformed them into a beautiful master bedroom/bathroom suite with hardwood floors and all new furniture and fixtures, connected it by hardwood stair to the upper flat, demolished our current bathroom, built two gorgeous new bathrooms, blew out most of the upstairs walls and reframed the building to create a "great room," and then made up for those lost offices by shoring up the foundation and reframing and finishing both the attic *and* the basement.

Cost estimate? They had no clue, but they thought it "probably wouldn't be *that much.*" Poor Liz got her hopes up and tried to find a contractor willing to bid on the "the whole shebang." But Contractor Number One looked around the house, looked at the Master Plan, asked how much we thought we were going to spend, heard us say, "Oh, I don't know, thirty grand?" and nearly spit on us. He said we were looking at a half-million-dollar re-model for which we'd have to move out for a year. Liz, growing desperate, begged me to sign off on just taking out a second mort-gage and going big; I told her this would be madness, given that we had neither retirement savings nor college funds for the girls. Liz came to her crestfallen senses and we tried, instead, to hire a journeyman carpenter to build the stair alone. But that failed, too: nobody wanted the job. So again I proposed building the stair myself. Liz agreed, and that was that: time to shelve the cookbooks, hang up the apron, and buckle on the old tool belt. I was not a good enough chef to satisfy myself; I was not done, emotionally, with that pursuit; but I felt clearly that I had to put more of my energies into activities directly benefiting the family.

I'd only just begun the project—power-sawing a giant hole into our current bedroom's floor, blowing my daughters' minds and making room for the staircase—when I drove to Berkeley for my first meeting with Alice. Despite my father's judgments, and even my own frustration with Alice's books, I wondered during the drive if I should see this as an acceptable end point to all my Alice study: not becoming a great cook on my own terms, nor even learning the core kitchen wisdom that could make me a better-adjusted human being, but rather joining Alice's office team as a minor player, a lesser courtier in my hometown's most exclusive society. I found a parking spot between Saul's Deli and the Bank of America branch at which Mom had given me that diamond wedding ring. Then I stepped under the Chez Panisse arbor and opened the hallowed door. I climbed the same stairs I'd climbed with Jane on my first dinner date, and I paused at the bar from which Ted, my father's law partner, had kindly treated my sixteen-year-old date and thirteen-year-old self like adults. Then I saw Alice herself, smiling as she approached: surprisingly petite, dressed in the pretty flowing fabrics of the affluent Berkeley-woman-of-a-certain age. She was an attractive and radiant person, and her eyes had the brightest of twinkles, absorbing all of me, sizing up a young man and deciding he dearly needed a cold glass of Domaine Tempier Bandol rosé. She took a booth for the two of us, and then she ordered a lavish lunch for me: pizza, pork chop, fruit tart, killing me with kindness, showing me how lovely our partnership could be. The wine in particular, all the way from Provence, felt to me like drinking the Chez Panisse sacrament, the Blood of the Goddess, right on the altar itself. Starstruck, I lost control of my tongue, babbling about how much all this meant to me, and also about the Montessori thing, and how I'd done all this cooking, and on and on. Alice blanched—ruffled, I'm sure, by the reminder that she was old enough to have been the pre-school teacher to a now-middle-aged man, so I tried to save the conversation by lavishing praise on her cookbooks, but that didn't work either. I'd forgotten the old recipes-suck rule of the professional chef, by which my claim to zillions of ticked-off Chez Panisse recipes could only mark me as an amateur or, worse, a culinary stalker. She responded especially poorly to my mention of the *Chez Panisse Menu Cookbook*.

"Oh, but the recipes don't even work in that one!" Alice said, horrified.

Most of all, though, Alice didn't want a new sycophant. She hadn't brought me to lunch to celebrate my devotion, or to become friends. She just needed a writer for a speech, for occasional speeches in the future, and, as it turned out, for a book on the Edible Schoolyard, a fruit-and-vegetable garden she'd sponsored in the same public junior high school I'd attended as a kid. She described that garden with messianic fervor, every bit as determined to change and save the world as she'd been in her youth. I'm not a true believer myself—never been much for causes, however worthwhile—but I left that day with a handshake agreement and a good work assignment, and I got back to my home carpentry. Before I turned Liz's office into a proper construction zone, I'd realized, I had to build a new office in our basement—meant to be mine, in the long run, but great for Liz while I made a mess building the new stair. So I hired a young illegal immigrant off the street, a man named Antonio, from a tiny village in the jungles of Chiapas. I worked in the early-morning hours on my Alice assignments; I worked until late afternoon, with Antonio, in the basement; and it took an awful lot of wine, each night, to wash away all the filth, stress, and exhaustion of doing so much important work for which I had so little qualification—speechwriting, carpentry, job-site management conducted in a pidgin Spanish with a man who'd grown up speaking some ancient Indian language. For that reason, I suppose, and also because I was thinking in Alice's voice, several hours a day, my cooking slipped back toward comfortable terrain. I still couldn't bring myself to cook from Chez Panisse cookbooks, so I mined Alice's bibliographies instead, coming up with several obvious candidates: David, Olney, Roy Andries de Groot, Kamman. Beyond the bibliographies, Alice's books were peppered with names both famous and obscure. The famous tended to be diners, like the Dalai Lama. The more obscure names tended to be farmers, ranchers, Chez Panisse employees, and cookbook writers (never other restaurateurs). People offered up as props, in other words, populating the quasi-fictional Chez Panisse universe, allowing Alice to invoke various ideas and feelings. There was Bud Hoffman, the birds guy; Bob Cannard, with his farm just outside the Bay Area and the vision he offered of a farm-to-table continuity, of funky Chez Panisse trucks banging up to the farm full of compost and returning full of greens; there was that Chino family farm, down in Rancho Santa Fe, a place of miracles; there was Olney, paragon of excellence and judgment, conferring approval; Kermit Lynch, too, the great wine importer with the funny name I'd seen emblazoned on a nondescript Berkeley building throughout my childhood (*Sesame Street* meets "Strange Fruit"); but, chief among them, exerting a curiously powerful influence, was this Lulu Peyraud. So I picked up *Lulu's Provençal Table*, a cookbook for which Olney spent a year taking notes in his dear friend's home. Alice's foreword offers that "the Peyraud family's example has been helping us find our balance at Chez Panisse for years. Like them, we try to live close to the earth and treat it with respect; always look first to the garden and the vineyard for inspiration; rejoice in our families and friends; and let the food and wine speak for themselves at the table." And then Olney's text and the photographs radiate the kind of French-countryhouse-culture porn so craved by my hometown, with its long opening essay on "The Vigneron's Year," conjuring this mythical natural-aristocratic existence in which the happy, loving winemaking couple and their children live and eat by the seasons and the changing of the vines, the aging of their own wines. But the recipes looked remarkably simple, and accessible—like pared-down versions of Chez Panisse recipes. So I began to give them a try: Turnip Soup was nothing but sliced onions salted and softened in oil, then slices of turnips (no greens required) warmed in the same way and covered with a little water and then a run through the blender and a sprinkle of pepper and croutons, and yet, to my immense pleasure and surprise, Liz loved it. Like, she *really* loved it, maybe more than anything else I'd ever made. Same for a cabbage soup I made the next day, again without so much as chicken stock for the base: just cabbage, onion, potato, and carrot, chopped and simmered and served. Liz openly enthused, a reaction I treasured, but found confusing, too. I treasured also the reaction I got the next day, when I moved Liz's furniture down to the newly painted basement office, hooking up her computer, putting a flower in a vase, and winning a sweet, grand smile from her, as she settled in to write.

Not that the project went smoothly: the demolition of a single wall in Liz's older office, necessary for the framing of the new stair, revealed a dark truth. The wall had been made of garbage, quarter-inch Sheetrock nailed directly over ancient wallpaper fixed onto wide, thin wooden slats, probably from the Great Depression. I couldn't bear to cover it up with more Sheetrock, so I got Antonio to help me rip that garbage off every other wall in the room, and in my own office, until we'd ripped both rooms to the studs. This only exposed more headaches: substandard framing, no earthquake proofing, ancient knob-and-tube electrical wiring. I hadn't built a single step, and already I was looking at double the projected time and expense.

Liz grew fond of the basement hideaway, and Antonio was thrilled—he'd stumbled into serious long-term employment. I bought a large library of DIY home-improvement books; I found helpers, including a plumber and an electrician who agreed to work on a consulting basis, giving pointers and supervising my finished work, and also a few neighborhood contractors who hadn't yet learned to run when they saw me coming, and therefore got interrogated almost daily. Then came the morning when I picked up Antonio at our usual spot and he got in my truck sobbing and reeking of alcohol. He told me that his sixteen-year-old wife had died, back in Chiapas; their baby daughter was even now with Antonio's mother. I delivered Antonio several blocks away to an older brother he'd never mentioned before, a vaguely scary-looking guy named Florentino, and I didn't see Antonio for a few days. When Antonio returned, he brought a second hitherto unmentioned brother, Nico. Nico turned out to be an absolutely terrific guy, equally hardworking, more skilled, and constantly cheerful and upbeat. When Antonio left for Chiapas, to be with his daughter, I bought him the new pair of basketball sneakers he wanted as a farewell gift, and I let Nico bring the elder Florentino, known as Tino, on board.

But *Lulu's Provençal Kitchen* provided just the right outlet: I didn't much care if I completed the book, but I did care that it gave me a way to please my wife, and I liked how quickly it let me assemble nice meals. I liked also the new window it gave me into Alice. Meeting with her every couple of weeks, I'd become fascinated by what an unusual person she'd turned out to be: always breathless, always agitated, eternally confessing to an awful hangover from some fabulous party the night before. She must have been in her midsixties by that point, and yet every time I saw Alice she mentioned dancing until all hours and drinking too much fabulous wine, as if Willy Bishop and Jeremiah Tower hadn't been aberrations after all; as if she remained the buoyant, playful hedonist of the *Chez Panisse Menu Cookbook*.

Alice met Lulu, I learned now, in precisely that period—after meeting Olney for the first time, during his 1974 publicity tour for *Simple French Food*. He still lived in the Provençal village of Solliès-Toucas, and he didn't come to California often, so Alice invited him to dinner, while Jeremiah Tower was still her head chef. A few months later, she was graced by a visit from Lulu and her husband, Lucien Peyraud, Olney's neighbors back in France and the proprietors of Domaine Tempier, whose wines Chez Panisse already sold. The Peyrauds lunched at Chez Panisse with Gerald Asher, their American importer, and Alice was so taken with them that, the following summer, she rented a country home near them in Provence.

During one of her first meals there, at Olney's home, Olney served Alice the Salad Tasted Around the World: "full of Provencal greens that were new to me," as she put it, "rocket, anise, hyssop." Given that rocket goes also by the name arugula, making this moment analogous to Michael Jordan's first encounter with a basketball, it's worth a pause for an uplifting detour into this luncheon's impact on the future of the American salad—jumbo bags of arugula and "spring mix" sold at Costco across the land. (Although, to be fair, Nora Ephron insists that some measure of the credit goes to her own best chef-friend from the period: "You can't really discuss the history of lettuce in the past forty years without mentioning Craig [Claiborne]," she writes. "He played a seminal role." Around the time Ephron moved to New York, apparently "two historic events had occurred: the birth-control pill was invented and the first Julia Child cookbook was published. As a result, everyone was having sex, and when the sex was over you cooked something. One of my girlfriends moved in with a man she was in love with. Her mother was distraught and warned her that he would never marry her, because she had already slept with him. 'Whatever you do,' my friend's mother said, 'don't cook for him.' But it was too late. She cooked for him. He married her anyway. This was right around the time that arugula was discovered, which was followed by endive, which was followed by radicchio, which was followed by frisée, which was followed by the three *M*'s—mesclun, mâche, and microgreens—and that, in a nutshell, is the history of the past forty years from the point of view of lettuce.")

But right there, in the story of Lulu, I found the wellspring for the post-Jeremiah, post-Bacchanalian image that Alice had created for the more mature Chez Panisse, the Chez Panisse of local, seasonal, and sustainable, such as I'd found in *Vegetables*. Alice once remarked that she'd originally chosen the name Chez Panisse after a character in Marcel Pagnol's Fanny Trilogy, "to evoke the sunny good feelings of another world that contained so much that was incomplete or missing in our own." Alice meant by this, she says, "the simple wholesome good food of Provence" and the web of genial human relations found in a more traditional society. Five years after that choice of names, upon joining Olney for lunch at the Peyrauds', Alice writes that she "felt as if I had walked into a Marcel Pagnol film come to life. . . . Warmhearted enthusiasm for life, their love for the pleasures of the table, their deep connection to the beautiful earth of the South of France—these were things I had seen at the movies. But this was for real. I felt immediately as if I had come home to a second family."

The Fanny Trilogy, it bears mentioning, entirely set on the urban Marseille waterfront, contains neither the wholesome good food of Provence nor any connection whatever to the beautiful earth. And Lucien Peyraud, far from being some Provençal peasant, had actually been born in a city of well over a hundred thousand residents called Saint-Etienne (sister city, Des Moines, Iowa), a center of coal mining and, later, bicycle manufacture, to a family that worked in the city's oldest industry, dealing in silks and ribbons. He had a twin who went into industrial engineering, and Lucien himself studied agriculture and then viticulture. Lulu Tempier, for her part, came from a Marseille mercantile family (granted, same town as the Fanny Trilogy); her father owned a leather-importing business that had been in the family since before the French Revolution. She was an art student. After she married Lucien, he worked on a big commercial fig farm and then took a job in

Lulu's father's leather business. Only after the French capitulated to the Nazis did Lulu's father give the couple Domaine Tempier, a family country property at which all the grapevines had long since been torn out for peach trees. The Nazis came through looking for homes to requisition, but when they knocked at Domaine Tempier and found the pregnant Lulu surrounded by three small children, with no electricity or running water, they went elsewhere. After the war, Lulu and Lucien worked hard turning their Domaine into a successful winery, and Lucien agitated for Bandol's declaration as an *Appellation d'origine contrôlée*. Lulu, in Olney's book *Lulu's Provençal Table*, remarks that "I hope the reader won't imagine that I never do anything but cook," and so Olney tells us that she became an impassioned sailor, and the Domaine's primary promoter, traveling France and even America to visit restaurants (Chez Panisse included, no doubt) and to place her wines. She received guests, so that her life was, in part, a performance; she was a cofounder of L'Ordre des Dames du Vin et de la Table, an association of French female vineyard owners.

Alice, in other words, had transformed Lulu and Lucien into the living embodiments of an already idealized France Alice had seen on the silver screen, and yet I found a certain relief in learning this. Faulting her for it, however, would be like faulting Mark Twain for embellishing certain details about the denizens of Hannibal, Missouri. At her core, Alice was a myth-maker, a culture-creator, a dreamer of beautiful dreams. Also, the Peyrauds did become dear lifelong friends to her, as well as muses, Neal Cassady to Alice's Jack Kerouac—the authentic ones, living out the authentic life toward which the self-conscious artist can only aspire. Extra-virgin olive oil, for example, from olives grown right on their property; herbs and fennel from the garden behind Lulu's old country home, or growing wild on the hillsides; green almonds and figs "from [Lulu's son] Jean-Marie and Catherine's house," as Alice put it many years later, in her introduction to *Lulu's Provençal Table*, a book she had personally urged Olney to write. "If the guests are very lucky, François will have been diving for sea urchins. Lulu searches for what is alive, knowing that that is always what tastes best."

I set out for the markets with new intent: for Lulu's Bourride, I took Hannah and Audrey both—aged four and two, by then—to a fish place. I taught them both to look at the gills and the eyes, judging freshness. Untroubled by recipe-ticking stupidity, I even enjoyed the markets more, focusing on Hannah and Audrey instead of some tick-list of required ingredients. After Lulu's Baked Bream with Fennel, Audrey actually drank the juices from the baking dish, spooning them up like fish soup, standing on a chair in her pink nightgown, fresh out of a bath. Liz reminded me, in this period, of what she'd told me several times in the early days of our courtship—how she wanted a simple life, disliked fuss or complexity in anything, least of all food. She talked again about recoiling from the ornate, feared entrapment by the formal, wanted the freedom to care about whatever she authentically cared about. She'd felt too often pressured, as a little girl, to care about formality in food when it meant nothing to her. And she wanted to know that my cooking of Lulu's food conformed to those yearnings. ("La cuisine de bonne femme," writes John Thorne, in his introduction to *Lulu's Provençal Table*, "the cuisine, that is, resulting from the interaction of a gifted home cook with the techniques, ingredients, and classic dishes of the local terroir. The unique combination of ravishing sensuality and moral integrity that is the core of good French cooking.")

Spring turned to summer, Hannah turned five, and then, one morning, Nico and Tino banged on my front door earlier than usual. I pulled on pants and answered and they said gently that they really needed the entire thousand dollars I owed them all at once, as in *right that second*. (They preferred to be paid in chunks, on very particular days; local gangbangers have a slang term for Mexican day laborers: they call them ATMs.) Parked in front of my house, as it turned out, was a sinister-looking van driven by a people-smuggler who had just brought, yes, a *fourth* brother across the border; if the boys couldn't produce a thousand dollars, they couldn't have Carlos.

So that's how my crew grew to three, shortly before the completion of that beautiful new bedroom, with its nice walk-in closet. So Carlos was there when I showed Liz around. She admired the gleaming hardwood floors. She congratulated herself on an excellent color scheme for the paints. She positively exulted over the walk-in closet, and I thanked her for having lived all those years without any closet at all. (Our only bedroom closet had been on my side of the bed, so it had only made sense, in my view, for that closet to be my closet.) Then Liz poked her head into that putative office nook.

Thinking aloud, Liz said maybe that cute little room ought to become a TV nook, and maybe she ought to stay put in the basement office that I'd created for myself.

"What about me?"

Maybe I should, well, you know, go back to the original plan and just stick a desk somewhere else in the basement.

I loved Liz's appreciation for the work I'd done, but I didn't much like this vision of my future writing space, so I found a solution during the following weekend, when Liz took Audrey and Hannah up to Napa. I was working alone on the one little adjustment we'd agreed to make upstairs, in our main living quarters: our single bathroom was ridiculously large, given the size of our home, so I knocked down one of the bathroom walls, to shrink it and thereby claim a little space for our puny dining room. But once I'd done the initial demo, and stood there in a pile of dusty debris, I realized that if we completely eliminated that bathroom, relocating the tub and sink to the putative TV nook, we could create not only a truly generous dining room, but a really proper master bedroom suite. And, once we got started really digging into the upstairs, it would be crazy not to rip out still more walls and ceilings and transform the unfinished attic space into a truly excellent little writing garret for myself. So I did, just like that; by the time Liz and the girls returned from Grandma's place in Napa, I'd turned that finishing-touch "move one last wall" project into a more-or-less complete gutting of our entire upstairs flat. And here was the funny thing: this amounted to the "whole shebang," the grand remodeling dream she'd always wanted, and I was on track for delivering it at a fraction of the price, in a fraction of the time, as we lived in the house.

When I did, after months of our children inhabiting what a friend called a "toddler death zone," we jointly discovered something about Liz herself, and that old relationship between suffering and desire. We'd discovered that she'd been right. (Or, as she put it, "that I'm not a spoiled little bitch after all, despite whatever you thought.") Because she really did stop hating our house, when it was all over. In fact, she loved the place, right on down to the attic office, which she claimed for herself. (I've since regained it; long story.)

I finished the remodel weeks before my fortieth birthday. We threw a big party with Lulu's menu for a Grand Aioli, and it was only a month later that Alice invited me to her home for the final editing session on that Edible Schoolyard book. As it turned out, she lived not a mile and a half from where I'd grown up, only blocks from my junior high school. One of the more striking things about Alice, to my mind, had always been how little she appeared to be motivated by money: influence, perhaps, and connection to influential people. But she had never opened another restaurant, never branded a line of kitchenware, never designed frozen dinners or anything else. And she wasn't even a majority owner of Chez Panisse, and therefore couldn't be making a mint from it; plus, she put all of her speaking fees right back into the Chez Panisse Foundation, funding more of her pet projects. Her house confirmed the implied values: the same Berkeley bungalow she'd inhabited for more than thirty years. After all that time, the great Alice Waters hadn't even moved higher into the Berkeley Hills, toward the more fabulous views. In fact, her place had no views at all, and very little natural light. Like all Berkeley Arts and Crafts bungalows, Alice's home had copious exposed wood, all very dark and soft-toned, muted and reassuring, and her kitchen had recently been redone with a nice touch: a counter-height fireplace for cooking, modeled on Lulu's own.

Before we settled down to work, Alice asked if I was hungry: "Shall we have a little lunch?"

"I'd love a little lunch."

Off she went, to see what she could offer. "Unfortunately, I have nothing but eggs," she said. "Do you like eggs?"

"I love eggs."

"He loves eggs. They're great eggs, too. They're from Soul Food Farm." She stood a moment, staring at me, tapping a finger on the counter. Then, with a sparkle, she said, "I'm going to have to make the Egg."

"The Egg?"

She nodded. "And that means I'll have to make a fire." And like that, she did: she quickly piled and lit some wood in that kitchen fireplace, the counter-height elevated one. While the wood burned down to embers, Alice opened her refrigerator and brought out a colander full of greens from her backyard garden, all picked by a gardener. She rubbed a garlic clove around the inside of a wooden salad bowl, and then she poured in a little vinegar, salt, and olive oil to whip up a dressing. When the embers were ready, Alice found a copper spoon the size of a ladle, with a two-foot handle. She rubbed olive oil inside the bowl of the spoon, then cracked an egg into it and reached the egg into the fire, setting it just over the wood embers. In moments, the egg puffed up like a soufflé, and Alice pulled it back out. Then she slipped it onto a piece of grilled bread, on my plate, sprinkled on sea salt and ground on some black pepper, and set some of that salad alongside.

I have since heard that Alice cooked the Egg in the very same manner for Maira Kalman, cartoonist for the *New Yorker*, and also for Lesley Stahl, on *60 Minutes*, and while that did make me feel a little less special, it was still the most delicious egg I'd ever eaten in my life, seasoned with stardust from an authentic personal hero, and she poured me a glass of Domaine de Fontsainte rosé, too. I don't like to drink at lunch, but I drank anyway.

We talked as we ate, and Alice allowed conversation to roam for the first time; I told her of my rapture with *When French Women Cook*, and she said that it was among the five most influential books in her life. I mentioned Lulu next, and Alice lit up still further, happy to be on common ground, escaping the tension of our unequal relationship. The other books she'd so loved, she said, were an Elizabeth David text, two from Richard Olney, and one I did not know, *The Auberge of the Flowering Hearth*, by Roy Andries de Groot. Alice then searched her shelves for—and could not find—a copy of de Groot. She phoned her office and asked that one be ordered for me, another for herself. But the point here is that Alice talked about all of these people; she told me about going to Annecy with Madeleine. She told me that Madeleine was very difficult, that she obsessed over book sales and felt horribly jealous about the success of others. Alice said that Olney, in particular, bothered Madeleine, and I recounted the scene in *When French Women Cook* in which Madeleine describes meeting Olney and being unimpressed—although this was precisely the tour in Burgundy that impressed so many other French experts. Alice talked about Julia Child, too, and knowing her, and I basked for those fleeting minutes in a sense of connection.

Alice prepared a pot of tea then, and while she waited for water to boil I took a risk: "Just out of curiosity," I said, "what would *you* cook if you had fresh peas, asparagus, fava beans, and artichokes? Just as a for-example?"

What I did not tell Alice was that, only the night before, I'd found the very same ingredients in my own fridge. Having long since cooked every relevant Chez Panisse recipe, and also every relevant Lulu recipe, I'd realized I would have to improvise. Sweaty with fear, I'd begun by cooking each ingredient in the manner most common in the Chez Panisse books: for the peas and asparagus, blanching in boiling water; for the artichokes, low-temp stewing in extra-virgin olive oil; for the favas, a little of both. And then, because I'd seen recipes with similar conclusions, I'd tossed everything together, moistened them with a little chicken stock, and declared the result my first Spring Vegetable Garbure.

The question I'd asked Alice, therefore, was a test—or, rather, a covert request for the correct answer to a test I'd already given myself, the one called "What would Alice do?"

Alice, unaware that she was setting me free, outlined precisely the moves I'd made on my own.

11
Gluttony as Heroism

"Voracious appetite," Montanari tells us, has long been linked to "a physical and muscular concept of power." In the early Middle Ages, when a tribal chief had to be the strongest and bravest man in town, he displayed this "animal-like, even bestial superiority" in part through hunting wildlife, but equally in his gorging on the kill, asserting his right to the greatest portion. Montanari argues that all this faded in the later Middle Ages, when "the nobleman was no longer *only* the warrior, and physical strength . . . no longer his most important attribute." With an increasing value placed on courtliness, according to this line of reasoning, "the sign of nobility henceforth was no longer the capacity to eat in quantity, but rather (and above all) the ability to know how to distinguish the good from the bad, and ultimately to master self-restraint and self-control." Far from vanquishing the old order, however, this new prissiness has come simply to coexist with it in our minds, such that even in the middle of the last century you could have the infinitely discriminating A. J. Liebling refer to "the heroic age before the First World War, [when] there were men and women who ate, in addition to a whacking lunch and a glorious dinner, a voluminous *souper* after the theater." Jack Nicholson might have been expressing disapproval when he quipped to Jim Harrison that "only in the Midwest is overeating still considered an act of heroism," but he recognized the idea's persistence none-theless. Same for Frederick Exley, in the opening pages of his magnificent novel *A Fan's Notes*, when Exley-the-narrator (as opposed to Exley-the-author; it's complicated) refers to a weekend of "nearly heroic" drinking. All of these men, I believe, express the widespread feeling that extreme gastronomic self-indulgence, however you judge it on moral terms, can indeed display certain of the attributes classically associated with heroism: bravery, daring, courage, spirit, fortitude, and boldness, say, if not quite gallantry, selflessness, or valor. It's that quality of letting go, giving free reign to one's essential nature, taking a risk and throwing off constraint; it displays the individual's willingness to do what everybody else only wishes they had the guts to try.

There's a quality of self-congratulation in this, too: no less an observer than M. F. K. Fisher, in *An Alphabet for Gourmets*, says she "cannot believe that there exists a single coherent human being who will not confess, at least to himself, that once or twice he has stuffed himself to the bursting point, on anything from quail *financière* to flapjacks, for no other reason than the beastlike satisfaction of his belly." Fisher doesn't see anything wrong with this, openly pitying, as she does, anyone "who has not permitted himself this sensual experience, if only to determine what his own private limitations are, and where, for himself alone, gourmandism ends and gluttony begins." Having deeply enjoyed these indulgences, in whatever rare instances we've undertaken them, we carry thereafter the warm glow of having said, in essence, *Fuck it, I'm going in*, and that colors the way we look at others doing the same. As for the *G* word, I believe that gluttony has lost considerable power for the reason cited by Francine Prose, in her monograph *Gluttony*. This particular sin, she points out, doesn't appear anywhere in the Bible, nor does it hurt anybody but the glutton.

And yet, early Christian thinkers were borderline obsessed with gluttony, considering it the gateway sin toward the hard stuff like anger, envy, and lust. To explain this, Prose conjures the delightful possibility that austere living conditions at medieval monasteries were to blame: so many single men, so little food, so much pent-up rage to vent toward any poor brother prone to grabbing that one extra bread crust.

Still, even today, it's one thing to permit yourself genuine gut-busting consumption; it's quite another to make it happen. The food has to be just right, the mood and the company, just so. In my own life, for example, it took a rare and never-to-be-repeated confluence of emotional currents and controversial health hypotheses, starting with my sense that a dive into Elizabeth David and Roy Andries de Groot would qualify as a retrograde movement of the soul, a burrowing back into the cultural warmth of Mother Alice. With Fergus likewise behind me—as much as I loved his food, I felt now that even he would discourage me from replicating it slavishly in the soft California sunshine—I felt my first-ever itch to study the mainstream American male celebrity chefs. Not just Keller, either. In a single order from Amazon, I bought used copies of Eric Ripert's *Le Bernardin Cookbook*; Joël Robuchon's *The Complete Robuchon*; Mario Batali's *Babbo Cookbook*; Tom Colicchio's *Think Like a Chef*; *Jean-Georges: Cooking at Home with a Four-Star Chef*, by Jean-Georges Vongerichten; and, on a whim, Harold McGee's *On Food and Cooking: The Science and Lore of the Kitchen*. Flipping through all these books, in a kind of culinary speed dating, I couldn't decide which to embrace first. Jean-Georges offered an introduction to Asian flavors; Colicchio presented fundamental techniques in a clear, cogent fashion ideal for home practice; and *Le Bernardin Cookbook* began with a curious account of the deep love between Maguy Le Coze and her late brother, Gilbert Le Coze, with whom she'd founded Le Bernardin. Black-and-white photographs showed the two, as children, in France, kissing romantically, open-mouthed. ("When I fuck Maguy, you cannot call it incest; it is love," Gilbert once joked to friends, according to a 1994 *New York Magazine* article about his heart-attack death at age forty-nine.) As for McGee, it was less a book to work your way through than a go-to reference for any time you couldn't figure out why an emulsion kept breaking. ("Every man I know who cooks seriously owns McGee," writes Jane Kramer, who claims that she, personally, is "less interested in how things work than in how they taste and whether they taste perfect. And never mind the theories that would have me the victim of some late-capitalist delusion that it's possible—indeed, my American birthright—to put a purchase on perfection, or even of some embarrassing religion of self-improvement.")

I still hadn't settled on a new Kitchen God when I discovered that nearly every one of these men—along with several other famous chefs, including Michael Mina and Guy Savoy—had restaurants in nearby Las Vegas, where fancy food had recently replaced topless girls as the blockbuster sucker-draws for casinos. I could just jump on a plane, in other words, and experience all their culinary styles at once. Then I discovered something else: because Vegas was Vegas, a foreign country where steak is the national food and where American men feel powerfully disinhibited in the opening of their wallets, several of those restaurants were in fact high-end steakhouses: Batali's Carnevino, Wolfgang Puck's Cut, Jean-Georges's Prime Steakhouse, Michael Mina's Stripsteak. Even the Michelin-starred French places, eponymous Temples of Gastronomy from Joël Robuchon and Guy Savoy, were offering wildly ambitious (and expensive) American beef, with which they never would've bothered in a different town. The world's greatest-ever concentration of culinary talent, as far as I could tell—including many guys I wanted to study—was engaged in a steak-cookery death match. And that's what I mean about the conditions being right for extreme exploration of my gustatory limits: if I'd merely set out to sample marquee dishes in all these places, I might've eaten daintily, fancying myself a food critic. Even on a seafood mission, or a foie gras mission, the protein itself would've encouraged a certain self-control. But steaks are different, rivaled perhaps only by genuine barbecue in their power to provoke pathological behavior.

I still don't think I would've gone to the wall—to the very edge of catastrophe—if not for a chance encounter with my father and two lawyer buddies of his before I left. It came about because my father fell twenty-five feet at a rock-climbing gym, landed on his ass, and blew out two vertebrae in the middle of his back. When I arrived at the hospital, my father wore a hospital gown and he lay perfectly flat and still and he suddenly looked so very old, so frail, as if in a dress rehearsal for death—an emotional preview of how it might feel to lose him. He'd made an embarrassing mistake, he told me: tied the climbing rope into his leather pants belt instead of his harness. High up on the wall, he'd leaned back to rest on the rope and the belt ripped. I wanted to yell at him for being so reckless with *my father's life*, and yet it was so like my father, so like myself: absentminded, losing keys, leaving half-filled coffee cups everywhere. He showed me that he could wiggle his toes but that nerve damage kept him from lifting his left foot upward. He was on a lot of pain medication, and he had to spend several weeks in the hospital, to stabilize his broken back, but it turned out to be a curious blessing.

With my father strapped down and sedated, and eager for company, I finally convinced him that my cooking emerged not from some inexplicably domestic—and therefore unmanly—aspect to my character, but from precisely the obsessive streak that had him studying bootleg tapes of the great flamenco Diego del Gastor, who'd never left his home village and never consented to being recorded, but whom the cognoscenti recognized as the finest flamenco guitarist of all time. Knife-sharpening got us started, and I did feel my father's attention wane briefly, as if wondering what had happened to *his son* if *his son* cared about something so mundane and, worse, *so tragically practical* as a kitchen knife. But the mood improved as I moved toward the lunatic element: "I mean, now I've got like three different wet stones constantly in a pot of water, I'm reading about metallurgy and stropping techniques and I'm all into this guy who's apparently a reclusive knife-making genius, replicating the ancient Damasacus blade-smith techniques."

"Isn't that it?!" Dad said, laughing on his hospital bed. "It's got to be like only twelve guys in the world even know about your guy. Why are we like this?"

We heard a knock on the room door. Then it opened and we saw his friend Gene, a rail-thin divorce lawyer and weekend musician with the stooped hep-cat carriage of the veteran jazz man. After Gene, a guy named Blumberg stepped into the room—huge, florid, a bon-vivant golfer with a white convertible Mercedes, gorgeous shirts, and bone-white hair swept beautifully back from his tan forehead.

"Danny!" said Blumberg, in his deep, kind, booming voice, eternally charming an imaginary audience. "What a pleasure to find you here!"

"Hey, fellas."

After a few preliminaries with my father—How's the food?

Nurses treating you okay?—Blumberg turned again to me. "Your dad tells me you're quite the cook, these days."

I smiled.

"Well, tell us. What's next? What's your next big food adventure?"

I hadn't yet confessed the Vegas trip to my father, and I felt nervous about doing so: he just wasn't a Vegas guy, and Liz's father, Doug, had signed up to come, as had my old liquor-exec buddy, Jon. I thought the Doug part might hurt my father's feelings, given that he and I had not been away together since our climbing days. So I watched my father's face for disapproval as I said I'd gotten this magazine assignment to eat every top-drawer steak in every one of nine white-tablecloth restaurants in the course of thirty-six hours, while quizzing each and every chef on how they worked their magic: As Liebling once put it, articulating the boundaries in which a culinary researcher must operate, "Each day brings only two opportunities for field work [lunch and dinner], and they are not to be wasted minimizing the intake of cholesterol. They are indispensable, like a prizefighter's hours on the road." With this in mind, I'd confronted the fact that eating only a single lunch and a single dinner per day would force my mission into a tedious, dreary, interminable week in Sin City. If I doubled up, however, or even tripled or quadrupled up, I could turn the whole mission into a culinary blitzkrieg.

I told my father and his friends also about my developing theory that Vegas was a place that simply had to exist somewhere on earth, so fundamental were the human hungers on which it thrived—Greed, Lust, and Gluttony, the Fun Three of the Seven Deadly Sins. (Who'd build a resort based on Hate, Wrath, Envy, and Sloth?) But what made Vegas so peculiarly American, I told my father and his buddies, was the crazed free-market competition for a piece of the action. Back in the 1950s, this meant opening a gambling hall and selling cheap steaks only to watch the next guy start paying his cocktail waitresses not to wear shirts; so now you're flying over to Paris and importing an entire French titty show, except then some other casino's putting up a three-hundred-foot neon sign the suckers can't miss. And so on, until you've got exact replicas of the Eiffel Tower competing with the entire Manhattan skyline and full-scale pirate-ship battles in which huge British sailing frigates genuinely sink in vast man-made lagoons, despite the fact that we're in one of the driest places on earth.

Gene and Blumberg, it turned out, were old Vegas hands, and they'd been going there since the days of the all-you-can-eat buffets, but they'd also watched the big change in the late 1980s, when Steve Wynn figured out that high-class restaurants were yet another way to wow the yokels—especially if the chef had done some time on TV. One thing had led to another, and Vegas had become a nonstop culinary talent show with unlimited funds, with nearly every big-name American and French chef lured into opening at least one Las Vegas restaurant, sometimes several. The de rigueur Vegas meal had remained the big steak, but all these culinary geniuses, motivated by a perpetually spree-spending male clientele, were now engaged in a decentralized, unplanned, unmonitored, and yet nevertheless world-historic celebrity-chef death match to create the finest, most decadent, most luxurious beef steaks ever experienced by humankind.

This was not a gross overstatement: the newly built $2 billion Wynn Hotel and Casino, to name a single casino, had both the Country Club (self-billed as the "new American steakhouse") *and* SW Steakhouse, which offered a 42-ounce chile-rubbed double rib eye for $98—a single portion of which could have provided a generous and fairly typical half-pound steak portion to each of five hungry men. Slice it up for stir-fry, throw in some broccoli, and you could feed a Laotian village. But only a block away, at the even newer $2 billion Palazzo Hotel and Casino, fully three of six brand-spanking-new restaurants were also wildly ambitious and expensive steakhouses. Morels, a so-called French Steakhouse, whatever that meant, offered, among other things, a 10-ounce "A-5 Wagyu strip steak frites with parmesan & truffle *pommes frites* and foie gras butter," which was about as turbocharged as pure steak decadence could possibly get and doubtless somehow still a bargain at $185. In any other city, that dish would have qualified Morels as the go-to beef-lover's temple par excellence, but Morels was absolutely outclassed *within the same casino*, by Wolfgang Puck's CUT, where the appetizers included Kobe steak sashimi, Prime sirloin steak tartare, and bone marrow flan, and where the steak list offered the discriminating carnivore the opportunity to compare corn-fed Illinois Prime dry-aged twenty-one days with corn-fed Nebraska Prime dry-aged a full thirty-five days, and to compare a crossbreed of Japanese Wagyu and American Angus with purebred Japanese Wagyu, just to be sure you were on top of the key distinctions.

"The way I see it," I told those guys, in the hospital room, "the very future of steak is currently being defined in Las Vegas, and it's my duty to go eat it."

My father did look a little nonplussed by all this bullshit, and he made a light joke about cholesterol, but I was ready for this, too: my own cholesterol had been rising for years, I confessed. And I knew also that "grassfed" was a dirty word in Las Vegas steakhouses, and that I would therefore be gorging on the equivalent of morbidly obese adolescent animals slaughtered moments before they would've expired from their own toxic adiposity. But I'd been reading Pollan's second food-related bestseller, *In Defense of Food*, at about that time, and I'd come across his chapter about the lipid hypothesis, the whole idea that saturated fat clogs the arteries, causing heart disease and turning us into fat people. To be fair, Pollan begins *In Defense of Food* with his now-famous exhortation to "Eat food. Not too much. Mostly plants." But I'd been much more excited by his dazzling midbook endorsement of yet another book that I'd run out and bought: *Good Calories, Bad Calories*, by Gary Taubes, a monumental assassination of the lipid hypothesis. All over the world, according to Taubes, eighteenth- and nineteenth-century British colonial doctors working with hunter-gatherer peoples eating their traditional diets had observed a total absence of the diseases of civilization—obesity, diabetes, heart disease. These doctors had also observed, however, that any time hunter-gatherer groups moved into a colonial capital, adopting a Western diet, they quickly came down with all of these ailments. As for the cause, well, their traditional diets had ranged from the Masai's eating nothing but cow's blood, milk, and beef to Eskimos living on seal blubber, so the dietary culprits behind the diseases of civilization simply could not be cholesterol or saturated fat. Taubes then documented, with almost pathological thoroughness, the shoddy science that had made the link between saturated fat, cholesterol, and heart disease in the first place. The overwhelming preponderance of evidence, Taubes demonstrated, pointed rather at foodstuffs universally absent from hunter-gatherer diets but ubiquitous in the Western world: flour and sugar. As a meat-loving man with dangerously high cholesterol, I took this to be the best dietary news ever delivered to mankind. So long as I cut out the cookies and the bread—the stuff that was actually killing me, in other words—I could devour all the meat I could stomach, at every single meal, and I didn't even have to worry about how happy the animals had been, before the bolt gun punctured their crania.

Gene and Blumberg positively loved this rap. Plus, they knew all about the great chefs I hoped to meet: Savoy, Robuchon. They'd also tasted enough Kobe beef to understand the big price tag at a lot of these restaurants. This, in turn, gave my father the joy of seeing old buddies engage with his son, even throwing out their own anecdotes of excess, like one from Gene about snorting Russian caviar through a hundred-dollar bill, at a Scottsdale golf resort.

I countered with a fabulous meal I'd eaten recently with Liz, at a two-Michelin-star place called Cyrus, where a caviar cart cruised constantly among the tables.

"Wait," Blumberg said, "are you not aware that I'm an investor in Cyrus?"

I was not.

He looked lovingly askance at my father. Then, to me, he said: "And how about Gary Danko?"

I drew a blank. I knew Gary Danko was among the finest restaurants in San Francisco—my in-laws had taken me there—but I had no idea why Blumberg was mentioning it.

"Your father has not told you that I'm an investment partner in Gary Danko."

"Dad," I said, "how could you not have told me these things?"

My father laughed, enjoying the reprimand.

Blumberg said, "And what about you, Danny? Have you ever thought of opening a restaurant?"

"Ah . . ."

"Well, you should. You certainly could, you know? It's only a matter of financing. And I bet you'll learn a lot in Vegas—perfect research! I think we ought to talk when you get back. Go out in the city, huh? I could hire a car. We'll eat in all my favorite places. I'll show you around, you know? Introduce you to some people."

As I drove home that day, I thought of a line from Bill Buford's book *Heat: An Amateur's Adventures as Kitchen Slave, Line Cook, Pasta-Maker, and Apprentice to a Dante-Quoting Butcher in Tuscany.* Mario Batali asks if Buford wants to open a restaurant of his own, and Buford realizes that he does not: "When I started, I hadn't wanted a restaurant," he writes. "What I wanted was the know-how of people who ran restaurants. I didn't want to be a chef: just a cook. . . . I didn't want this knowledge in order to be a professional; just to be more human."

But even if I didn't follow up Blumberg's financing offer, I knew I would feel grateful for the way he'd celebrated my cooking love right in front of my father. It emboldened me to share more about all this with my father, and it helped my father to be more receptive, especially on the night he came back from the hospital, shortly before my Vegas trip. After weeks of institutional foods, fluorescent lights, and those bare-assed hospital gowns that make you feel like an incontinent baby, he got carried into the home by a team of medical-transport guys. My mother had rented a hospital bed and paid to have it installed in the downstairs den, among my father's banjos and guitars and poetry books, so that he wouldn't have to climb the stairs while his back healed. He was still suffering torrential nerve pain, shuddering agonies that swept up and down his left leg, leaving him speechless with pain, but at least he was surrounded by his own walls, with his own wife as the only nurse he needed. I made him the best steak I could, that night—a so-called Outside Skirt Steak, or Bavette, with caramelized shallots from a recipe in *Bouchon*. I poured my father a good

California Cabernet, too, and he savored it all like nobody had ever savored a meal of mine. And while I watched him chew every bite, the meat and wine reminding him that he was still a man, with grand pleasures still ahead in his life, I realized that he'd always been my most important audience, the only person who could truly validate my obsessive tendencies. Mom celebrated them, to be fair, and she always let me know that she admired the results, but only my father was similar enough in nature to help me believe that my compulsions came not from dysfunction or narcissism but rather from a healthy impulse to find joy and curiosity in everyday life.

So that's the spirit I carried to Las Vegas, allowing me to kick off the mission, only hours after our plane touched down, by ordering every money-shot steak available at Bobby Flay's Mesa Grill, deep inside the Caesars Sports Book. With the calm, serene confidence that I would survive the test ahead, I led the boys onward to Jean-Georges Vongerichten's Prime Steakhouse, at the Bellagio, where we showed up for the first of that night's dinners, and for the trip's first bite of Japanese A5 Kobe, the single most expensive and high-status animal protein consumed by humans (roughly $400 per pound retail, for filet mignon). Taken from the Wagyu breed of cattle raised in the Kobe region of Japan, A5 is the highest pedigree for Kobe beef. Mystery shrouded the exact breeding and rearing techniques, which were carefully guarded both by the Japanese Agriculture Ministry and by the handful of small ranchers who actually produced A5 Kobe, but various reports described cattle in total confinement and darkness, serenaded by soft music to keep them absolutely relaxed, with their weight supported by belly straps, and feeding eternally on beer and rice, with regular sake-rub massages to soften their muscles. The result was less like fat-marbled meat than like meat-marbled fat, or like some entirely different food you've never dared dream might exist.

"May I recommend a small-batch American bourbon, perhaps?" This was our Prime waiter's opening move.

"Hey, I've got a question for you," replied my friend Jon. "What's your view on pairing whiskey with beef?"

"Well, sir, the conventional wisdom holds that a properly grilled steak, with a properly charred exterior, can support a whiskey neat." He paused to clear his throat, and it was obvious the man loved the theater of all this. "But if, on the other hand," he continued, "you're considering a more subtle cut, such as a filet mignon, it's generally considered desirable to add a little branch water."

"Branch water?"

The waiter laughed. "Creek water. Just, you know, *water.*"

Then the A5 arrived and melted my face. Before I get lost in describing it, let me say that it was only a nibble compared to what followed: a 10-ounce New York strip, a 16-ounce rib eye, and an 8-ounce filet, accompanied by sides that included truffled mashed potatoes and by an assortment of steak sauces: a peppercorn sauce with brandy; another with soy, rice wine, and roasted garlic butter; a classic béarnaise, with herbed butter; and an Asian-inflected sauce with lemon zest, lime zest, orange zest, and grated ginger.

But back to the A5, because it was the big news. It was offered first as an appetizer: we each got four thin slices on a white plate, paired with balsamic preserved portobello mushrooms stuffed into a Japanese shishito pepper. And from the moment I placed the first slice in my mouth, I felt as though I'd eaten the red pill in that movie *The Matrix*, clearing out the delusions we all take for reality and exposing our life as it really is. That A5 Kobe, in other words, turned out to be the most transporting single bite of food ever to pass between my lips, with a paper-thin crispy exterior yielding to such oozing and sumptuous fats that I felt as if I'd discovered a whole new pleasure organ within my own anatomy. (Brillat-Savarin: "The creator, while forcing men to eat in order to live, tempts him to do so with appetite and then rewards him with pleasure.")

And sure, I began asking questions, picking up a few tricks. Cooking a pro-grade steak, I learned from the Prime chef, a guy named Robert, required the reconciliation of opposing demands, one for hell and one for heaven: hell because it took the fires of damnation to char flesh in the manner demanded by true steak aficionados, and heaven because only the slowest and gentlest of warming could possibly produce the tender interior that looked equally pink from just under the crust to the very center, and that still oozed with natural juice and blood. The basic trick was and remains hitting your meat first with high heat, searing the surface, and then lowering the heat to let the interior "come to temperature" more evenly. But the chefs of contemporary Las Vegas were pushing so hard at this core program that Moore's ceramic broiler roared at a terrifying 1,200 degrees, allowing him to char the steak's exterior before the interior even noticed he'd pulled it out of the fridge. And yet Robert was already upgrading, convinced he could get even more extreme and instantaneous charring out of a new 110,000 BTU infrared broiler capable of hitting 1,800 degrees, the temperature at which jet fuel burns, and also at which certain grades of steel begin to melt.

So the moment he got your order, the Prime grill chef yanked the meat out of a refrigerated drawer, covered it with salt and pepper, and slipped the whole slab into the blast furnace for about three minutes. Once he liked the color he was getting—the dark brown exterior—he pulled that steak out and shoved it into a 600-degree convection broiler. Three minutes flat and now the interior was up to rare, so he hauled it out again, squirted on a thick layer of melted butter, ground a pile of black pepper on top of that butter, and shoved it back into the super-broiler, where the butter instantaneously foamed up, absorbed all that pepper flavor, cascaded down the sides of the steak, and then browned to a crunchy hard bark. Steaks are cut from muscles that contract in reaction to intense heat, toughening up and squeezing all their juices toward the center, so the final step was a resting period, a few minutes away from high heat so the steak could relax again, becoming more tender and redistributing moisture. Then the plate was on its way to your table.

Dashing out of Prime, having wolfed that whole meal in under forty-five minutes, we then trotted burping across a pedestrian bridge and slipped into Caesars for a reservation at Restaurant Guy Savoy, the eponymous eatery of the Michelin-starred French gastronomical artist. Apparently, when the casino bosses first came calling upon Mr. Savoy in Paris—"Okay, Kermit, name your price. What is it, ten million? Twenty? All we want is an exact copy of this here joint"—Savoy père had tapped his son, Franck, to head up the new project. So it was Franck we met, and Franck to whom we directed our questions about steak cookery.

"You can't really want to talk only about beef at Guy Savoy," he said.

"I'm afraid we can."

"But in Paris, we don't even serve beef."

"Why not?"

"The quality of French beef is no good."

"Couldn't you just fly in American beef? People ship fresh fish all over the world."

"This would be very hard for the French clientele, to say you are using American beef in France. We would be dead."

He looked disgusted, so I asked why he bothers to serve steak here, in Vegas.

"Hey, we are not stupid. No steak, no client."

Then his waiters delivered flutes of Champagne and quite a load of new A5, every bit as face-melting as the stuff from Prime: slices accompanied by a sweet onion purée, and sliders on toothpicks. Moments later, after we'd inhaled all the A5, out came Savoy's "American prime beef tenderloin and *paleron à la française*," which was essentially a pairing of a French pot-au-feu with a big filet mignon topped by bone marrow. And where Vongerichten nuked the exterior of a steak to satisfy the Inner Caveman, Savoy took the opposite approach: only lightly searing the filet's exterior, in a pan of hot grapeseed oil, and then simply lowering the flame beneath this pan and adding a bunch of butter.

"Our palate is not so aggressive," Franck explained. "It is more subtle."

We were surprised, however, by how quickly this American-char-versus-Gallic-finesse distinction collapsed at our very next restaurant, our final meal of that first night: at Stripsteak, inside the Mandalay Bay, where chef Michael Mina had a truly innovative steak-cooking technique. Just behind the grill, there was a long stainless-steel table with multiple rectangular openings in the top, each sized to hold a deep rectangular pan. Once set down into the tabletop, each rectangular pan was warmed from below by a separate bath of heated water, its temperature controlled by an independent digital thermostat, with one dedicated to each pan. These gently warmed pans were then filled with enough melted butter and fresh herbs to completely submerge even the biggest of steaks. ("It's like a warm marinade," Mina told me.) In order to skip that whole seize-up effect, from extreme heat, Mina used this process—a fusion, really, of industrial *sous-vide* and the old-world oil-poaching technique for preserving fish—to slow-poach his steaks for as long as three hours, never bringing them above 110 degrees, which was just below rare. All day, in other words, long before you even found the restaurant, your steak was drifting in a state of blissful suspended animation, changing ever so slowly. This way, when your order came in, your beef was already just at the brink of rare and yet profoundly, soulfully relaxed—so much so that the quickest of kisses on a mesquite grill would sear up the pre-warmed surface and pulse just enough heat through the meat's middle to make the whole thing perfect and also to make a man understand that, despite the glories of A5 Kobe, good old American Black Angus does have its moments.

All my life, I'd wished I could make myself vomit. I could always find the button, no problem: it was right at the back of the throat, that slippery-but-hard knob you could press, triggering the gag reflex. But no matter how stuffed and bloated I got, and no matter how hard I rammed my whole filthy hand down my own gullet, I could never quite evacuate my belly. Coaching was doubtless the missing link—puke coaching, I mean, of the kind M. F. K. Fisher once gave to James Villas. Having driven to Napa to interview the great lady, Villas became hideously ill from bad oysters he'd eaten in San Francisco. While he moaned and spewed in M. F. K.'s bathroom, she kindly alternated between interviewing herself ("Well, my friend . . . when I was a young lady, I learned how to cook and make love; when I reached the age of 50, I learned how to treasure friendship and grow old; now I'm learning how to die") and giving Villas tips like "You must not simply lean over the bowl . . ."

But that didn't stop me from trying in the gleaming granite beauty of the bathroom in my room at Caesars—gagging and drooling while my old friend Jon and my father-in-law hung out at the blackjack tables. When I gave up and lay alone atop my bed, oozing saturated fat and alcohol from every pore, I realized that I had in effect turned my mouth into a meat grinder and my body into a sausage casing—a human hog-intestine, jammed to bursting with what the British call forcemeat. I got confirmation of this when I stepped onto the bathroom scale at midnight. For the first time ever I'd broken two bills, and I thought of Montanari's other great point about meat-eating—that vegetarian motivations are "doubtless the expression of a will to reject a life-style of carnivorous eating culturally long synonymous with the exercise of power, force, and violence. Denying oneself meat means distancing oneself from the enticement of power. It was not coincidental that the majority of monks issued from noble lineage. In their 'conversion' a reversal of eating habits played a prominent role. The symbolic importance of renouncing meat is reflected in the monks' preference for 'poor people's food,' borrowed from the peasant world as a sign of spiritual humility: greens, vegetables, grains."

It goes without saying, of course, that our putative grain-eating poor man craves nothing so much as that nobleman's rejected steak, and I found my own culinary allegiances shifting right back to the Social Register by the next day, over lunch at the Delmonico Steakhouse, Emeril Lagasse's operation inside the Venetian, where my father-in-law announced that he'd won $1,100 in forty-five minutes the prior night. I felt a curious ache in my belly that I finally recognized as—could it be?—hunger. We tore like champions through a bone-in New York strip, a filet mignon, and a bone-in rib eye—all accompanied by house-made potato chips flavored with (gulp!) black truffles and Parmesan. And, just for good measure, we devoured some New Orleans BBQ shrimp.

"Non! Non! Non!" This was super-chef Joël Robuchon, a few hours after the Delmonico feast. He was standing in the red velvet cocktail lounge of his eponymously named MGM Grand restaurant, Nevada's only three-Michelin-star dining establishment. Dubbed "the Chef of the Century" by a top French culinary review and the possessor of a total of seventeen Michelin stars, the most held by any living chef, Robuchon looks and dresses like an avant-garde international architect, a severe intellectual in a black turtleneck and black plastic eyeglasses, and I'd provoked him by asking if he, like all other chefs, salted and peppered his meat before cooking.

"Non! You must salt the meat only *while* it is cooking and after, but *never* before." Salt draws out moisture, was the point; moisture is golden.

So what about pepper?

"*Only* once the meat is cooked. This is because the flavor of pepper changes intensely with heat. The only exception is for steak au poivre, and even here, you would never, ever add salt before pepper."

Why?

"Because the moisture the salt pulls out will release the pepper. So: for au poivre, pepper first. Then salt."

I loved this guy. He was clearly out of his mind.

And sauce?

"Je suis *contre* le sauce!" he barked, like a Trotskyite terrorist opposing bourgeois reforms to the Communist Party Platforms.

Robuchon's translator interrupted, to clarify: "Monsieur Robuchon would like to explain that he is opposed to sauce, *always*."

Not that Robuchon wouldn't drizzle a little *jus* over the finished steak, but where classical French technique often called for *jus* built around butter, vegetables, and red wine, Robuchon was a fierce minimalist. ("Pas du vin! Pas du vin!" he shrieked. "No wine! No wine!") Trimming a raw steak of all its imperfect fat, gristle, and stray meat, Robuchon would sauté the trimmings in a small skillet until they were well browned. Then he would pour in just enough water to release those brown bits from the surface of the skillet and to barely cover the trimmings. Simmering this pure beef-water liason, Robuchon would then strain it, reduce it, add a little salt, and voilà!

The result, as we experienced on a 16-ounce A5 Kobe rib eye, the biggest single serving of A5 available anywhere in Vegas, was a miracle of pure beef flavor that, if I had to guess, must have clocked in at around $300. (In case it's not obvious, I paid for none of this.)

Our joy was tempered, however, at our next stop, another Michael Mina restaurant, when my father-in-law's BlackBerry picked up an e-mail from his cardiologist, answering his query about the possibility of a dangerous cholesterol spike in a single piquant word: "Yes." And we began truly to disintegrate at the stop after that, Tom Colicchio's Craftsteak, the second-to-last meal of our campaign and the scene of our first genuine filet mignon taste test: a 10-ounce USDA Prime filet ($56); a 10-ounce Wagyu beef filet from Snake River Farms in Idaho ($115); a 6-ounce filet of grade 10 Wagyu beef from the Blackmore Ranch in Queensland, Australia ($138); and an entire 6-ounce filet of grade 12 A5 Wagyu beef from Kagoshima, Japan ($180). A once-in-a-lifetime comparison opportunity that, at any other moment on any other day, would've elicited sobs of ecstasy, and this is all I heard out of Jon, the single worst influence I've ever considered a dear friend:

"I'm guessing porn stars."

"What?"

"Those chicks over there."

Thirteen women gathered around a nearby table: loose dresses falling off salon-browned shoulders, hair so teased wild it looked like they'd just crawled out of an orgy, reapplied their lipstick, and gone hunting for protein. "What's your guess?" Jon asked me. "Hookers?"

"For Chrissake, Jon, do you mind?"

Fortunately, Doug was asleep. Sitting next to me at our table, but asleep nonetheless.

As I began carving the steaks, a deep weariness settling over my bones, I found my thoughts drifting to ipecac, that vomit-triggering medication so beloved by adolescent ballerinas. I began also to visualize a very private and very nicely scented toilet in some remote desert spa, followed by a Zen wheatgrass enema tenderly delivered by a smooth-skinned young woman with a foreign accent. And I might have drifted away altogether if my father-in-law hadn't snapped me back.

"What'd you say?" I asked, because I hadn't heard properly.

"Australian Wagyu," he muttered, chewing something.

"Yeah?"

"It's the . . ."

"What's that, Doug? What'd you say?"

It was no use; he'd fallen back to sleep, leaving Jon and myself to confront the problem with two pounds of world-class filet—namely that, no matter how much meat you've already eaten, it's

still two pounds of world-class filet. It turns out that it is physio-
logically impossible *not* to eat two pounds of world-class filet,
when they're juicy hot on a plate below your nose. So we did,
every bite, and most of the sides, and even though I felt certain
I was killing myself, I was still shoving wild mushrooms and
spinach soufflé into my mouth when we waddled off toward the
Last Supper at Mario Batali's Carnevino, our ninth and final
restaurant.

Like the decaying salon of somebody's aristocratic Italian great-
grandfather's dusty and ancient castle, Carnevino had an inexplicably gaudy and massive gold-painted statue of a bull near the front
door. Then our waiter, apologizing for the fact that the 36-ounce
rib eye would take forty-five minutes to cook, absolutely insisted
we share a little salad, just to tide us over.

"Oh, no!" I shouted. "I mean, totally unnecessary."

Jon: "Yeah, we're good."

Waiter: "Don't worry about a thing. You're going to love it."

As if awaiting our execution, we sat in fading silence until the
salad arrived. Without meaning to, I served myself exactly one
leaf. The leaf sat alone on my plate as I stared at it and grew desperate at the very idea of consuming it. So I cut my one leaf in
half and then folded the smaller half onto my fork and exercised
fierce willpower in bringing it to my mouth. And then, inexplicably, we began to order more. A plate of beef carpaccio emerged,
accompanied by warm lardo crostini: thin-sliced raw beef, in other
words, with cured pork fat on toast. Steak tartare followed, with
enoki mushrooms planted as if the fungus had sprouted directly
from the raw meat—a somewhat dubious aesthetic implication—
and there was an element of thrill in how much I liked this stuff.
And how much of it I actually wanted to eat.

Thrill turned to giddiness when that rib eye arrived—it was

about the size and heft of your average garden-path flagstone—on its own cutting board, perched on a cart alongside our table.

"So, how much do you guys know about aging?" asked the chef, Zach Allen.

In truth, we'd gotten quite an introduction, because every Vegas restaurant was making a big deal about it—claiming, by and large, that their beef went through about three weeks of "wet aging," in which it sat around inside vacuum-sealed plastic bags, and another three weeks of "dry aging," meaning the meat hung in the dry air of a cold meat locker. The idea behind aging is that once an animal dies, naturally occurring muscle enzymes begin assaulting and destroying other cells, breaking long, flavorless molecules into shorter, tastier bits, and also dissolving some of the connective tissue between the muscle fibers, tenderizing the meat. Dry-aged meat also dehydrates over time, concentrating its remaining flavor but causing about a 20 percent loss of product, both because of moisture loss and because the exterior becomes so rotten and mold-covered that much of it has to be cut off and thrown away. For obvious reasons, supermarket beef and even most meat at butcher shops is never aged at all: nobody wants to lose poundage in a dry-aging process, and even wet aging requires you to tie up inventory and pay power bills while the meat sits around in some refrigerated warehouse. And even high-end Vegas steakhouses generally buy meat that has only been wet-aged long enough to start that enzyme work without losing weight, and dry-aged only long enough to capture that concentrated flavor.

But at Carnevino, we learned, they were doing the things the hard way.

"See, the cattle are slaughtered on a Monday morning," Chef Allen told us. "We have a USDA inspection, and the very next guy to touch the beef is our guy, and he'll stamp it with our brand. Then it comes to us on Thursday night and never goes into a cryopack. It goes instead into a thousand-pound box called a combo that we keep at thirty-five degrees with eighty-five percent humidity, and with a lot of air movement. There are a few other tricks, too, but the main thing is that we can now age our meat for a hundred and twenty-four days."

Four months?

"That meat you're about to eat, that's how old it is."

Roman emperors would have long since crammed entire living peacocks down their throats, hoping to purge. High Seas pirates could easily have abandoned us to a lifeboat without oars or food in the South Pacific only to hear that we'd washed ashore a month later in Tasmania, insisting to befuddled locals that we craved only a light salad. Our caloric needs hadn't just been met, they'd been eliminated into the foreseeable future. And yet, because I'm not a quitter and also because I didn't want to hurt Chef Allen's feelings, I lifted my steak knife one last time, reached deep for strength, and carved off just one itty-bitty teeny-tiny bite. Placing that morsel on my tired-out tongue, and summoning the will to chew—and wishing also that Chef Allen would scram so that I could spit it out—I felt a confusion creeping into my mouth. Chewing a little longer, and readying my wineglass to receive my ejected cud, I meditated a moment and then located the source of my perplexity: this meat tasted like no other in Vegas. So, instead of spitting it out, I washed it down with a sip of Cabernet and carved off another bite.

Gamy and nutty, in an old-world, Roquefort-cheese kind of way, Batali's magnificently rotten beef wasn't just delicious, it was sensational. Jon and my father-in-law, working on their own big mouthfuls, were both looking at me now, smiles breaking across their nodding faces so that even at this absurdly late hour, when a solitary leaf of lettuce had almost been the straw to make these three camels projectile-vomit, we dug in yet again, calling to the waiter for, yes, even more wine.

12
Recipes Are for Idiots Like Me, Take Two

Every student—or at least every insecure student, like myself—needs a master, a gatekeeper to answer that all-important question, "Am I any good at this?" Sometimes our gatekeeper appears in one of the obvious guises: my father, for example, teaching me to climb safely, and then authorizing me to climb alone; or my graduate-school adviser, signing off on my doctoral thesis. At other times, after studying something privately in the messy imperfection of daily adult life, we have to foist the gatekeeping job onto unwitting victims, like I did with Thomas Keller. Not initially, of course: after the *Bouchon* tragedies, I forgot about Keller for several years. He only came back onto my radar when I happened to read Michael Ruhlman's memoir *The Making of a Chef*, in which Ruhlman claims to have gone to culinary school for method, not recipes, because "recipes were a dime a dozen." Having thereby devalued the only culinary currency I'd ever hoarded, Ruhlman said he'd wanted to learn, instead, "the classical preparation of stock, the foundation, the bedrock of classical cookery. If you didn't know how to make a great stock, if you didn't even know what a great stock tasted like, you were doomed to mediocrity in the kitchen, at best, and at worst, ignorant foolishness." Given that I'd never even thought to taste one of my own stocks in isolation, and that I'd certainly never tasted a professional's stock, I faced now the very real possibility that I suffered from both mediocrity *and* ignorant foolishness. Nor did it help when Ruhlman went on to say, "If I didn't know how sauce Robert worked—perhaps the oldest sauce still in use—if I didn't know the qualities and behavior of a demi-glace, the queen mother of French sauces, then truly I knew nothing."

I didn't have the slightest clue what sauce Robert even was, and for about ten seconds I contemplated going to culinary school myself, just to rectify the problem. Once that delusion faded— kids, money, the fact that I would've hated culinary school, even if I'd gone as a young bachelor—I figured that I should at least try mastering the aforementioned techniques at home. I bought a 20-quart pot, a fine-mesh conical strainer, a mountain of veal bones, and the Culinary Institute of America's gargantuan student textbook, *The Professional Chef.* Then I roasted bones and simmered bones and skimmed stocks and tasted stocks and, finally, froze stocks. Just for comparison, I made the veal stock from *The French Laundry Cookbook*, too, a wildly expensive and time-consuming process that produced both a magically concentrated elixir and the curious discovery that this Ruhlman character was listed in the book's credits, doubtless as the hired-gun writer. When I was done with all this veal stock, I bought Raymond Sokolov's *The Saucier's Apprentice: A Modern Guide to Classic French Sauces for the Home*, along with James Peterson's encyclopedic *Sauces: Classical and Contemporary Sauce Making*, and I got to work on that sauce Robert. But then I hit yet another roadblock: neither Liz nor I actually wanted to eat proteins with classical French sauces every night. It felt like a ludicrous way to live, and I was done with the idea of my cooking as, to quote Liz's favorite term from the period, "arts and crafts." I needed my cooking to produce food that our family would enjoy eating.

I was just growing desperate over this realization, and I was ready to give up on ever finding a trustworthy path toward becoming like Ruhlman and Keller, when Ruhlman himself lit my way home. In his second cooking memoir, *The Soul of a Chef*, Ruhlman describes the borderline-crazy testing process chefs go through in order to become something called a Certified Master Chef, or CMC. But he also describes Keller himself as the living embodiment of what that test strives to codify: total, unequivocal mastery of contemporary fine-dining cuisine, a kind of seventeenth-reincarnation of the Chefy Lama whose divine soul has remained perfectly intact through some unbroken chain of being that included Escoffier and even Carême himself. I learned, for example, that Keller had neither formal training nor extended mentoring, but he'd fallen in love with the simple trick of making hollandaise at a Florida yacht club, as a young cook. Over time, that love had blossomed into a broader passion for technique, a life-sustaining joy-in-process. Keller had preserved this joy right through his early career and into the very layout of the famous French Laundry kitchen: windows onto a garden, clean carpeting, soft music, a staff so calmly competent they moved in a kind of serene dance, never hurrying. Cooking well, as Keller described it, was "simply a matter of caring." Understand the method, and then execute. This attitude extended even to the smallest details: Keller apparently stored asparagus upright in water, to keep it fresh, green, and unblemished; he packed fish on ice in precisely the body position in which those fish had once swum the seas. Most of all, Keller worked "as if wanting to extend each task rather than finish it . . . wiping down his entire station after storing what he'd just prepared. He worked very clean so that as he began each preparation, it seemed to be the first of the day." Excellence doesn't begin with the plate, Keller told Ruhlman, "it begins when you wake up. It's got to be a philosophy. You have to be determined, determined to do it every day. If you're going to have a clean plate, you've got to have a clean oil bottle."

I was already quivering with the implied promise of self-transformation—*model your every waking second after my own example, and you, too, can begin the long, quiet march toward the Chefisattva state from which I currently experience Eternal Peace, Wisdom, and Badass Culinary Chops*—when a minor detail in Keller's self-description caught my notice. He tells Ruhlman that he prefers to be seen not as a celebrity chef so much as a "Buddhist monk in search of perfection," and I could suddenly hear my own father saying this very phrase, a wry, playful tone in his voice. I even recalled a story my father had told while standing dumbfounded inside my demolished home, during the remodel. He'd never swung a hammer in his life, never had the slightest interest, so he'd been horrified by my tangle of extension cords and the piles of shattered plaster on the ruined floors and the dust covering everything, raising very real questions about how his own son could've fallen so far from the tree as to enjoy such misery. But then my father had reached deep to say something kind. He'd offered a story about a "Japanese Zen carpenter," by which he meant not that the carpenter himself was Japanese, but that this man had studied "Japanese Zen carpentry," whatever that was, in Japan. (Zen was ubiquitous in Dad's tales, along with gypsies; Buddhism and flamenco being the yin and yang of essential manhood, for my father.) My father said he'd noticed this carpenter working away on an empty Berkeley lot. The heart of the story lay in the man's having taken advance delivery of all the lumber he'd need for the entire house. For weeks, he'd had done nothing but measure and cut every board for the entire building, piling them in tidy stacks according to the order in which he'd need them. Then my father's Japanese Zen carpenter put away his saw, took out his hammer, and assembled an elegant home.

As nice as all this was, however—as nice as it felt to fall in love with a fantasy version of this Keller guy—I couldn't exactly see how to emulate his perfection. Flipping through *Bouchon*, once again, I wondered if I should just suck it up and make all those frog's legs and rabbit terrines—all the super-Frenchy stuff I'd previously skipped, in deference to Liz. The food in *The French Laundry Cookbook* looked almost comically difficult, but perhaps I would have to go there someday, too. Salvation came in the very next Keller/Ruhlman cookbook production, *Ad Hoc at Home: Family-Style Recipes*, which happened to be published that very autumn. Replacing Keller's upscale French food with the Americana served at his casual restaurant, *Ad Hoc at Home* offered the perfect fusion of super-chefy excellence with food my family would actually enjoy, such as buttermilk fried chicken, prime rib, hamburgers, and iceberg salad with blue cheese. Keller himself appeared, throughout, in photographs showing him in casual street clothes instead of chef's whites—your new best friend in the everyday American kitchen. Whatever cynicism I might have felt toward this overt rebranding, it all vaporized when I read Keller's opening anecdote about how his father, in the last years of his life, had come to live in a small cottage next door to the French Laundry. Largely by chance, Keller says, he had the honor of cooking what turned out to be his father's final meal. Keller then offers instructions for replicating the menu: grilled chicken with bottled barbecue sauce; mashed potatoes; collard greens; strawberries and whipped cream with store-bought shortcakes. "I am unspeakably grateful to have made it—that dinner remains important to me," Keller writes, recalling also the food shared by grieving friends and family afterward. "Whether it's a sad or difficult time, whether it's an ordinary-seeming day, or whether it's a time of celebration, our lives are enriched when we share meals together," he says. "And that's what the food in this book is all about."

Under a photograph of Keller and his father, taken near the end of his father's life, Keller then introduces a design feature of *Ad Hoc at Home*, a sprinkling of kitchen tips and wisdom labeled "lightbulb moments." The first of these, Keller says, "is one I was lucky to realize in time, and hope that others will too. It may seem obvious but it's worth repeating: Take care of your parents." Because that lesson had been so important for me, personally—and because I had learned it by cooking the *Bouchon* skirt steak upon my father's return from the hospital—I read the rest of *Ad Hoc at Home* in a state of open-minded rapture like I hadn't experienced since *Chez Panisse Vegetables*, seven years earlier. In an essay entitled "Becoming a Better Cook," Keller appeared to speak directly to me, cautioning the home cook who tries to do too much, and who never cooks the same recipe twice. He suggested instead a saner path toward self-improvement: cooking the same meals repeatedly, so as to practice "the handful of tasks professional cooks do over and over." Gift of gifts, Keller then listed the actual tasks: roasting; sautéing; poaching, braising; big-pot blanching; using salt properly; using vinegar as a seasoning; roasting a chicken; making soup; and cooking eggs. After learning all of these techniques, Keller said, "challenge yourself. That is the way anyone—an athlete, a doctor, a musician—improves his or her skills. Set increasingly difficult tasks for yourself. Maybe it's as simple as focusing on slicing an onion thinner, or dicing vegetables more uniformly, or braising short ribs correctly, taking the time to understand the different ways that short ribs look and smell and feel throughout cooking." He ended with an admonition to "be organized," addressing the one remaining thing in my cooking that Liz still loathed. But here was the key that set me free: instead of pitching kitchen organization as a way to please the cook's neat-freak wife, Keller said that "good organization is all about setting yourself up to succeed. It means getting rid of anything that would interfere with the process of making a recipe or preparing an entire meal." Just like that, Keller provided all the rationale I'd ever need for embracing the core belief expressed by Liz and demonstrated daily by her mother, but which I could apparently hear only from Keller himself: that, as Keller put it, "being organized is the first and most important part of cooking."

I get a hot kind of adrenaline rush when I've got a new obsession, and that's how I felt as I banged out every *Ad Hoc at Home* recipe not just once but two or three times, taking care to practice every core technique, challenging myself like an athlete. I cut vegetables with a ruler, to make sure my half-inch dice was precisely half an inch. I roasted chickens and Rack of Pork Arista. I sautéed broccoli raab and I oil-poached sturgeon and I braised short ribs. There were soups and there was vinegar; there were even soft-boiled eggs. I never cooked a meal without a gigantic pot of boiling water for my daily practice of "big-pot blanching." I even salted my food in precisely Keller's recommended manner, grabbing big pinches of his recommended brand, Diamond Crystal Kosher Salt (in perfect accordance with Gopnik's assertion that "the salt fetish" is driven primarily by our desire "to bond with the pro cooks").

Soon, I'd developed a distinctive daydream in which somebody I'd invited to a dinner party would call moments before arriving, asking permission to bring a friend. This friend would turn out to be Keller, and I would be trussing a chicken to roast, from *Ad Hoc at Home*, when Keller walked in. I would not worry about the taste of my food because I would trust Keller to enjoy having a meal made for him in the warmth of a nice home. Instead, I would ache for Keller to notice that I was sautéing with a light touch and salting with my fingers and using vinegar to bring up the acid profile. I would ache, in other words, for the Seventeenth Chefy Lama to smile that beneficent Zen Master smile and say what Yoda says to Luke Skywalker in *The Return of the Jedi*: "No more training do you require. Already know you, that which you need." (Luke's reply, while we're at it: "Then I am a Jedi?")

Nora Ephron, I knew, had suffered similar cookbook-motivated crushes, including one on Craig Claiborne. Ephron writes of wondering what she'd even cook, if Claiborne ever came to dinner, and whether or not it should come from one of his own cookbooks. ("Perhaps there was a protocol for such things," she wrote. "If so, I didn't know what it was.") Claiborne did come for dinner, in the end, and Ephron even got invited to Claiborne's house, but it was her later obsession with a cook named Lee Bailey, whom she met through the gossip columnist Liz Smith, that felt so deeply like my Keller thing: "I became Lee's love slave, culinarily speaking," Ephron writes, admitting that he "replaced all my previous imaginary friends in the kitchen. . . . I began to osmose from a neurotic cook with a confusing repertory of ethnic dishes to a relaxed one specializing in faintly Southern food." Then, the clincher, proving we're all a bit alike: Bailey, Ephron confesses, "was, in his way, as close to a Zen master as I've ever had."

Ad Hoc at Home turned into a bestseller, winning awards and forcing me into the classic psychology of the fan: believing there to be something special about your own fandom; insisting, to yourself, that you loved the hero way before he became huge (utterly preposterous, in the case of Keller and myself); imagining even a deeper understanding of the artist than other fans could possibly share, and feeling certain the hero could recognize this understanding, if only you could meet.

We did finally meet, when the magazine for which I worked asked me to put together something called Five Meals Every Man Should Master. The idea was to find a chef who could teach us, in exquisite detail, five meals to cover every key occasion in a guy's life, from the hot date to the poker game. For reasons I still do not understand, Keller agreed to be that chef. I'd been a journalist for a long time, and I'd never really felt nervous about meeting my subjects. But I felt intensely nervous about meeting Keller because my magazine assignment was, first and foremost, a way to pass through those French Laundry kitchen doors on personal business, so that I could find a way to gauge if my skills were even barely adequate.

So I hardly believed it when I heard that "Chef" would spend two hours with me, from ten to noon, on a Monday, at the French Laundry. Chef "wondered" if I could stay for lunch and, if so, if I'd like to eat what we cooked together or, rather, if I'd like something sent over from the restaurant.

Were they crazy?

There was even a voice mail request about attire: Chef would like to know what he should be wearing. Casual? Or chef's whites?

I almost wept: Keller, asking me what to wear!

I left early on the appointed morning, constantly checking the traffic on my iPhone. I drove across the Bay Bridge, through Berkeley, and up toward Napa. I drove too fast and then I worried about crashing, or getting pulled over and thus arriving late, having to explain to Keller that I'd been arrested. When I got to Yountville and parked my crappy Subaru across the street from the French Laundry, a lovely young woman awaited me out front. Her name was Kristine, and she put me right at ease while leading me into the little white bungalow where Keller's father had lived. The bungalow still flew the American flag out front, along with a flag from the United States Marine Corps. We stepped through a small living room with simple furniture and a Bocuse d'Or 2009 commemorative object. Beyond that lay a sun-filled kitchen—not big—that I later learned to be an exact replica of the Bocuse d'Or competition kitchen. After his father died, Keller had had the home's kitchen redone as a Bocuse d'Or practice space: Keller himself had been selected as the American team's president that year; his French Laundry chef Tim Hollingsworth had beaten twenty-four other American chefs to be the team's head chef, and Keller had given him months of paid leave to practice.

Suddenly, I saw Keller himself, talking on his iPhone, tall and slender in his fresh chef's whites. He shut off the phone and gave it to Kristine and extended a hand while I set down my pile of his cookbooks. We'd already settled on our five dishes: Roast Chicken; that Bouchon Bavette Steak; Rack of Lamb with Asparagus; Pork and Beans; and a sandwich that Keller had earlier developed for the Adam Sandler character in the movie *Spanglish*, a BLT with melted cheese and a fried egg. Keller was instantly warm and friendly, but he was all business, too, asking what sort of recipes I wanted for this article. What format should they take? Should they be conventional, full-blown formal recipes? Or something simpler?

Before I could stop myself, I blurted out that I just loved the recipe format in *Bouchon* and *Ad Hoc at Home*, and that I'd personally found these recipes a great gift to the reader. I suspected instantly that I'd given the wrong answer—that Keller, like Alice, would chafe at a love for even his own recipes. Reaching up to a shelf, he flipped opened the cookbook he said that he'd found most inspiring in his own journey, Fernand Point's *Ma Gastronomie*. Looking through it with him, I found the recipes deeply worrisome in their sheer Frenchiness, and frighteningly imprecise. Oeufs à la Gelée, for example: "Poach 2 eggs for each person to be served, and prepare a jelly with pigs' feet and some veal and chicken bones. In the bottom of a mold arrange a little foie gras and the poached eggs. . . . Pour in the jelly, allow it to set, and serve chilled."

I broke into a cold sweat just *thinking* about all the unexplained techniques. (*Now, okay, wait, does he really want the pig's feet and the chicken bones fixed inside the jelly?*) But then Keller flipped to a less disturbing example, for Truffle Salad: "Brush and clean thoroughly some fresh truffles from Périgord. Slice them on a mandoline and marinate them for ten minutes in a mixture of lemon juice, salad oil, salt and pepper. Serve immediately with some foie gras on the side."

"See, I love that," Keller told me. "You have to have confidence to be able to do that. That's like two sentences! But it *becomes yours* precisely because it's not like, 'Take five hundred grams of truffle, add, you know, fifteen centiliters of lemon juice, it's none of that stuff. That's why this book was so beautiful to me; it allows *you* to be the chef." Keller told me that when he began writing *The French Laundry Cookbook*, he actually hoped to work in the same vein, creating a cookbook without recipes. His editor wouldn't have it, so he'd gone with the more traditional American recipe format—with a few exceptions that he wanted me to see. Keller then picked up my copy of *The French Laundry Cookbook* and I said, preemptively, so as not to be caught out, "That's the only one of these books I really haven't cooked from much. I've only made the veal stock."

Just as these words came out of my mouth, the book fell

open, in Keller's hands, to the veal stock recipe. He paused to look at it, knowing what a claim I'd just made. With a single finger, he pointed to a lone brown stain on the page: "Look at that," he said. "You really did make it."

Having failed a first imaginary test, by revealing my recipe-love, I was thrilled to have passed a second. When it came time to roast the chicken, therefore, I tried to double down by asking if I might truss the bird on my own, with Keller's supervision. I'd trussed dozens of chickens, by that point in my life, all according to the identical description offered in *Bouchon* and in *Ad Hoc at Home*. But Keller stopped me almost as soon as I'd begun.

He said, "Wait, is that how you understood my instructions?" Keller waved me aside, pulled my string right off the chicken, threw it away, and cut a fresh strand. Then he demonstrated a trussing technique I'd never seen anywhere. I was already deeply confused when Keller finished by tying a slipknot, something else I'd never done. Then he cut the string, untrussed the bird, offered me a piece of string, and told me to give it a try. I did fine, until that slipknot. Keller demonstrated—this loop, that strand, pull snug—and I tried it myself, and I failed. So Keller snipped off the string again, cut another length, and I tried again. I failed again. Instead of growing tense about the time, however, or frustrated by my dumb fingers, Keller appeared calmed by this, as if happy to recognize a genuine teachable moment, and to embrace it—as if he were thinking, *Ah, here we go, the real thing.* For exactly eighteen minutes of his life, Keller ignored everything in the world except making sure that I mastered a simple knot. When I finally did—when I finally got it right, and successfully trussed that chicken—he responded as though the victory belonged to both of us, and we could now carry on.

Something similar happened in our second cooking session,

at Keller's Manhattan restaurant, Per Se. We'd developed a certain familiarity with each other by that point. I'd faced up to the inescapable fact that people like me aren't even really cooks, to people like him. We simply cannot get the infinite hours of the requisite repetition, searing a thousand fish fillets a week, for years on end, or trimming fifty racks of lamb a day, every day. But Keller let me know, somehow, that he recognized and appreciated my love for even the smallest technical details of his craft. When it came time to make that steak, for example, at Per Se, Keller playfully insisted that I notice everything down to the way he tilted the skillet while flipping the meat, letting all that hot oil pool out of the way, to on one side, so it wouldn't spatter. When it came time to baste the steak, he plopped half a stick's worth of butter on top of the meat, letting it melt slowly and then foam into the pan. He tilted the skillet again, and then he set a smashed garlic clove into the butter, along with a rosemary sprig. Then Keller asked if I'd like to do the basting, spooning the butter from its pool up over the steak, keeping the topside of the beef warm while infusing it with flavor. Once I began, clanking that spoon against the metal pan, scooping up the butter, Keller laughed and took the pan from me.

"Listen carefully," he said, with an affectionate, teasing smile. The rhythm of his own basting—of his own spoon, clanking with each scoop of butter—had a distinctly faster and far more macho rhythm, almost like insistent knocking on a door.

"So what are you doing this weekend, anyway?" Keller asked me.

Right on the tip of my tongue was "Not much, want to get a beer?" But I said, "Nothing really, just hanging out."

I realized that we would soon part ways for good, and I wasn't quite certain that I'd gotten what I'd come for. So I said,

"Hey, can I ask you one last thing? I'd love your advice on where exactly I should go next, in my cooking. I mean, I've really cooked almost everything from *Bouchon* and *Ad Hoc at Home*. So maybe *The French Laundry Cookbook* next? I feel pretty ready for that."

In hindsight, I can see that I badly wanted Keller to say, "Absolutely, Daniel. Having watched you work in my very own kitchens, I can see that you've mastered the basics and you're ready for the next level. Onward, my son! Onward to greatness!"

But Keller thought about the question, doing me the honor of taking it seriously. Then he said, "You know what I think? I think you ought to just stick with the kind of food we've been doing together."

I felt stung, of course, taking this to mean that he didn't think I was ready for the French Laundry, that I ought to stick with the basics a little longer. At first, I ignored the advice. I found myself thinking about our Fernand Point exchange, and Keller's remark about how a recipe "becomes yours," allowing you to test yourself against it. As I understood this, Keller meant that a cook never quite absorbs a hyper-detailed recipe—having to return, always, to the book, and to the precise measurements. In that way, a cook never broke the recipe addiction, never trusted himself to create. Recipes like Point's, on the other hand, functioned more like a friendly voice saying, "Hey, why don't you slice up a few truffles and serve them with a piece of foie?"

That wasn't a recipe, see, that was a suggestion. Following it required filling in so many details that the finished product wouldn't be Point's in any meaningful sense; it would be yours. You'd also remember it—not as a recipe to look up, but as a move you'd once made, and could easily make again. I'm not drawn to poached eggs in aspic, and I knew I'd have to sell my old truck to buy a meaningful number of Périgord truffles, what with all my Oregon truffles long gone. So I devised a solution of my own: creating, for my own use, the *French Laundry Cookbook* that Keller had wanted to write in the first place. Keller, then, could become my own Fernand Point. Starting with a dish called Clam Chowder, I first followed every instruction, nose in the book. Then, a few days later, I made it again, but this time from handwritten notes I'd made in the spirit of Point: "Sweat open some clams in white wine and herbs, incorporate the juice into a cream sauce, spoon a little sauce onto each serving plate, and top with a pan-fried cod cake, then a piece of sautéed cod filet, and, finally, a 'chowder' made from the reserved clams." After making this dish a few times, I threw away even my handwritten notes. That's when the dish became my own—not because I could make it from memory, but simply because I knew how to sweat open shellfish, make a cream sauce, fry some fish cakes, and sauté filets, and I could now try this with any fish combination that struck my fancy.

Looking for another French Laundry recipe to master, however, two things happened: first, I discovered a small essay in which Keller described precisely the chicken-trussing method he'd taken all that time to teach me, complete with the slip knot. Learning that very technique, it turned out, had served as a critical turning point in Keller's own apprenticeship. It had also become a key metaphor in his vision of the culinary craft—exemplifying the foundational skills upon which all fine cooking depended. Perhaps I could tell myself that Keller, in passing this knot along to me, had paid me the only compliment that made any real sense: acknowledging my authentic desire to begin the real journey of the cook.

The second thing that happened, when I went looking for another French Laundry recipe, was that I couldn't settle on one

I wanted to prepare three times in a single week, with Liz for my only audience. Liz herself had no problem with it: I'd gotten my cooking so controlled, after those visits with Keller, that I no longer made much of a mess. Liz and the girls even enjoyed those meals, excessive as they were, for weeknight meals at home. My resistance to moving forward, I concluded, had to be coming from within, which made me rethink Keller's parting advice. Perhaps he hadn't really meant that I was unprepared to learn fine-dining cuisine; perhaps he simply knew that fine-dining cuisine didn't make much aesthetic sense for the daily life of a young family. The food I'd cooked with Keller—Ad Hoc food, in essence, the food I already knew how to make—very much did.

13
What We Talk About When We Talk About Our Last Supper

Anthony Bourdain's introduction to *My Last Supper: 50 Great Chefs and Their Final Meals*, a coffee table book edited by Melanie Dunea, argues that chefs, "more often than not, have dined widely and well. They know what a fresh white truffle tastes like. The finest beluga, for them, holds no mystery. Three-hundred-dollar-a-pound otoro tuna and the most unctuous cuts of Kobe beef are, to them, nothing new." As a result, Bourdain writes, when chefs play that parlor game known as My Last Supper, kicking around visions of what they'd want to eat before facing the firing squad, "we seem to crave reminders of simpler, harder times. A crust of bread and butter . . . poor-people food." Crusty bread does appear with impressive frequency in the fifty meals that follow, but so do all of the aforementioned luxury foods. Beluga and other caviars, for example, make Thomas Keller's list (a half kilo of osetra), Martin Picard's (a whole kilo), Jacques Pépin's (an even ton), and also the lists of Hélène Darroze, Guillaume Brahimi, Anita Lo, and Charlie Trotter. Keller and Lo both like the sound of a little otoro, and truffles appear on the lists of Pépin, Eric Ripert, Darroze, Picard, Masa Takayama, Gary Danko, Jonathan Waxman, Scott Conant, Angela Hartnett, and Paul Kahan. Foie gras, that other marquee luxury food, pops up on the death-meal lists of

Darroze, Brahimi, Conant, Lo, and Picard, and as for Bourdain's reminders of "simpler, harder times," Jean-Georges Vongerichten wants "a royal banquet at the Grand Palace in Bangkok" in the company of the king of Thailand, while Mario Batali self-prescribes eight or ten seafood courses at an outdoor trattoria on Italy's Amalfi coast, in the humble company of international TV star Bourdain and Hollywood screenwriter and novelist Jim Harrison (as well as Batali's whole family, to be fair), plus live music from both an REM-U2 combo and a John McLaughlin–Paco de Lucía reunion. Bourdain's own last meal revolves around Fergus's signature starter, the one I'd eaten at St. John, in London: "Roast bone marrow with parsley and caper salad, with a few toasted slices of baguette and some good sea salt." You can't argue with the poverty associations there: Paleolithic campsites bristle with cracked marrow bones, including Neanderthal bones, early evidence of that eternal human impulse to eat the competition. But Bourdain wants this dish prepared by Ripert, Batali, Gordon Ramsay, and Fergus himself, right at St. John, a star-chef quartet inside the world's coolest restaurant, putting a distinctly non-poor-people spin on things.

No fault of Bourdain's: he was being kind, writing a characteristically brilliant introduction to somebody else's book, and he doubtless meant only to help when he posed for the book's photographer stark naked and smoking a cigarette, showing off his lean physique (truly impressive, and not just for a chain-smoking ex-junkie) while holding a cow's raw femur bone upright in front of his groin, like a twenty-pound erection, a great visual joke about the admittedly massive girth and heft of his own culinary cock deriving in large part from his personal outrageousness. Once again, to be fair: Bourdain cops to a certain discomfort with the photograph, offering that "I do always joke that (as some comedian once suggested) 'I want to leave this world as I entered it: naked, screaming, and covered with blood,' but . . . it's probably not wise to make career decisions after four shots of tequila." Also, if there is one predominant theme in these fifty final meals, it's a theme Bourdain would doubtless include, were he to write that introduction now, after his late-in-the-game marriage and the birth of his own first child: the near-universal desire to spend one's final moments among family and friends. True, Dan Barber—like the pre-kid Bourdain himself—pictures dining alone, and several other chefs lean heavily toward the company of dead people and complete strangers, like Charlie Trotter's yearning to spend that ultimate hour with Dostoyevsky, Hemingway, Bukowski, Henry Miller, Tom Wolfe, Hunter S. Thomspon, and F. Scott and Zelda Fitzgerald, a dinner crew he'd have more luck assembling shortly after that final meal, upon his presumed arrival in heaven, or at least in the outer circles of hell, where Dante himself described meeting many cultural luminaries. (Ditto for Marcus Samuelsson's guest list of Martin Luther King Jr., the food-hating Gandhi, and nobody else; and also for Martin Picard's sole invitee, Jesus Christ, whom Picard claims to want not because the opportunity to feed Christ at such a critical juncture might tilt His judgment, but because Jesus "is used to having a last meal," the Lord's life, being, apparently, a kind of divine Groundhog Day.) By and large, though, everybody wants precisely what I would want: wife, parents, siblings, dear friends, children, even if some chefs yearn like Gabrielle Hamilton to send the children to bed early, after dinner, letting them "fall deeply asleep so that I could eat quietly, contemplatively, and pretend that I was a single, younger person without intense, bone-crushing responsibilities . . . *sans* employees, children, or saggy boobs."

Fergus, likely one of the few chefs in *My Last Supper* to have properly contemplated the end—having stared down the gun barrel of major brain surgery—envisions a particularly beautiful and believable summer Saturday's luncheon, at home with his family, apartment windows open to the London street noises and "many platters of sea urchins washed down with Muscadet." Cigarettes play a prominent role—why not?—as do cheese, ice cream, and drunken dancing. "That should help soften the blow," Fergus says, capturing what I consider the essence of the exercise. The blow to which Fergus refers, I believe, is not so much the death blow itself—the bullet, the guillotine—but the blow of knowledge, the awareness of the end growing nigh. That knowledge is always with us, every day of our adult lives, flickering in and out of consciousness. Fantasizing about a final meal, therefore— menu, companions—amounts to thinking through our views on what softens the whole of the earthly passage, asking ourselves what matters most, and whether or not food even plays a meaningful role.

So here's my own dream of that Last Supper—or, rather, here's a representative supper, in the everyday flow of this family's changing life. Summer's cold and foggy in San Francisco, so I'm thinking about mid-September, when it always warms up a little. Audrey's six, a big first-grader. Hannah's nine, a third-grader, and I pick them both up at school, drive them home, and watch them run out the back door, down the steps I built. We've cut holes in our backyard fence, joining our little postage-stamp property to the neighbors on two sides. We share chickens with one of those neighbors, an ace rose gardener named Katy: the coop on our side of the fence the chicken run on hers, so the birds can move around during the day. But this time the girls slip into the other adjacent yard, climbing onto a big trampoline belonging to a seven-year-old boy named Cuya. I can hear them jumping and laughing and chattering with Cuya while I tie on my apron and whip up a little dinner.

We've finally stopped having separate meals for kids and grown-ups, and Liz now demands that the girls taste at least a little bit of everything Dad makes. The experiment shows promise. First time out, I made things easy by cooking my current go-to version of that old Odd Nights Pasta, based on the Garden Tomato and Garlic Pasta from *Chez Panisse Vegetables*—the one where you just heat up the olive oil with all that chopped garlic and then toss in the chopped fresh tomatoes and cook them until they relax. Ignazio, my recipe-hating Italian buddy, started cooking from *Vegetables* recently, and even he thinks Alice is onto something with that approach. I pushed the envelope a little on our second night of insisting the whole family eat the same meal, at the same time: I fried up a little squid, served it with a garlic mayonnaise. I watched with amazed eyes while Hannah actually ate a few rings, stomaching a food that, along with everything else from the sea, she'd always considered a vile form of poison inexplicably inflicted upon her by an otherwise trustworthy father. But Audrey, exploiting her sister's squeamishness, had gone nuts gobbling all the squid tentacles and telling Daddy that calamari was her new favorite food. So tonight, for Joint Family Dinner Number Three, with the girls on that trampoline and Liz out jogging, I'm trying to build on my success with a meal that falls somewhere in between. My thought is to light charcoal on the back porch, grill up a chicken—store-bought, of course, as I'm not allowed to eat the flesh of our own birds, only their eggs. But I've learned this trick of cutting out a chicken's backbone, spreading the body open flat, and then stuffing a little garlic-herb butter under the skin. Then you make slits in the skin at the base of each breast and tuck the drumstick ends into those slits to create a nice tight little package for the grill.

Liz gets home about the time the bird goes over the coals. She's showering while I'm making Caesar dressing and frying bits of bread for croutons. Then Liz opens a beer, sets the table, and calls the girls. What happens next only matters because it's happening to me: Hannah does her usual deal of demanding breast meat, Audrey takes a leg to have fun gnawing at a bone, they both load up on those croutons at the expense of the lettuce, and they happily eat the whole meal, with at least an outward appearance of gusto. It all tastes good to me, too, and somehow I start telling the girls that I cooked pretty differently before I got married, how I had this burrito system where I'd always keep black beans, brown rice, salsa, and guacamole in the fridge, along with big whole-wheat tortillas, so I could whip up a monster bellyful at a moment's notice.

Audrey's face brightens, and she says one of those amazing things kids often say. She says, "Will you make that for us, Dada?"

Knowing she's got me, and that my life has finally come full circle, I say, "Absolutely, kiddo. I'd love to make my old surfer-dude burritos again, just for you."

Like everything blessed in our lives, such moments are gone almost before we've noticed them. Hannah, for example, soon begins the nightly negotiation over whether or not she's eaten enough to get dessert. But just for once, I tell the girls not to sweat it, we're all going out for ice cream, no matter what.

ACKNOWLEDGMENTS

My agent, Sam Stoloff, played a critical role in shaping the idea for this book. Kathy Belden, my editor at Bloomsbury USA, was consistently kind, patient, and supportive, throughout the writing process. Certain portions of this book depended upon the generous support of magazine editors. At *Men's Journal*, these have included Will Dana, Jason Fine, Brad Wieners, Terry Noland, and Will Cockrell; at *Bon Appetit*, Hugh Garvey and Christine Muhlke; at *Food & Wine*, Dana Cowin, Pamela Kaufman, Michelle Shih, and Michael Endelman; at the *New York Times Magazine*, Ilena Silverman. At *Sierra*, Reed McManus and Steve Hawk. More than a few chefs have helped me along the way. These have included Alice Waters, Thomas Keller, Fergus Henderson, Chris Cosentino, Staffan Terje, Anne Walker, Sam Mogannam, and Daniel Patterson. My mother, Katharine Duane, not only cooked me countless loving meals over the years, but encouraged me to play that role for my own family. My wife's parents, Doug and Judy Weil, introduced me to the pleasures of fine dining, at more great restaurants than I can count. Ignazio Moresco, Joe Hefta, Brad Melekian, Bill Gifford, Michael Romano, and Kiernan Warble were all kind enough to read early versions of this book and promise that I wasn't making a complete fool of myself. My wife, Liz Weil, read pretty much every version and, together with my daughters, Audrey and Hannah, gave me a reason to cook in the first place.

SELECTED READING

Barnes, Julian. *The Pedant in the Kitchen*. London: Atlantic Books, 2003.

Bertolli, Paul, and Alice Waters. *Chez Panisse Cooking*. New York: Random House, 1988.

Brillat-Savarin, Jean-Anthelme. *The Physiology of Taste; or, Meditations on Transcendental Gastronomy*. Trans. M. F. K. Fisher. Berkeley: Counterpoint, 2000.

Chamberlain, Samuel. *Clementine in the Kitchen*. New York: Modern Library, 2001.

Colicchio, Tom. *Think Like a Chef*. New York: Clarkson Potter, 2000.

Fearnley-Whittingstall, Hugh. *The River Cottage Meat Book*. New York: Ten Speed Press, 2007.

Harrison, Jim. *The Raw and the Cooked: Adventures of a Roaming Gourmand*. New York: Grove Press, 2002.

Henderson, Fergus. *The Whole Beast: Nose to Tail Eating*. New York: Ecco, 2004.

Kamman, Madeleine. *When French Women Cook: A Gastronomic Memoir*. New York: Ten Speed Press, 2002.

Kamp, David. *The United States of Arugula: How We Became a Gourmet Nation*. New York: Clarkson Potter, 2006.

Keller, Thomas. *Ad Hoc At Home*. New York: Artisan, 2006.

———. *Bouchon*. New York: Artisan, 2004.

———. *The French Laundry Cookbook*. New York: Artisan, 1999.

Liebling, A. J. *Between Meals: An Appetite for Paris*. New York: Random House, 1995.

Montanari, Massimo. *Food Is Culture*. New York: Columbia University Press, 2006.

Olney, Richard. *The French Menu Cookbook*. New York: Ten Speed Press, 2002.

———. *Simple French Food*. New York: Wiley, 1992.

———. *Lulu's Provençal Table*. New York: HarperCollins, 1994.

Pellegrini, Angelo M. *The Unprejudiced Palate*. New York: Macmillan, 1948.

Ripert, Eric, and Maguy Le Coze. *Le Bernardin Cookbook: Four-Star Simplicity*. New York: Clarkson Potter, 1998.

Rouff, Marcel. *The Passionate Epicure*. New York: Modern Library, 2002.

Ruhlman, Michael. *The Making of a Chef: Mastering Heat at the Culinary Institute of America*. New York: Holt Paperbacks, 1999.

———. *The Soul of a Chef: The Journey Toward Perfection*. New York: Penguin, 2001.

Shere, Lindsey Remolif. *Chez Panisse Desserts*. New York: Random House, 1985.

Tower, Jeremiah. *California Dish: What I Saw (and Cooked) at the American Culinary Revolution*. New York: Free Press, 2003.

Trillin, Calvin. *The Tummy Trilogy*. New York: Farrar, Straus & Giroux, 1994.

Waters, Alice. *Chez Panisse Café Cookbook*. New York: William Morrow Cookbooks, 1999.

———. *Chez Panisse Fruit*. New York: William Morrow Cookbooks, 2002.

———. *Chez Panisse Menu Cookbook*. New York: Random House, 1982.

———. *Chez Panisse Vegetables*. New York: William Morrow Cookbooks, 1996.

Wrangham, Richard. *Catching Fire: How Cooking Made Us Human*. New York: Basic Books, 2009.

Ziegelman, Jane. *97 Orchard: An Edible History of Five Immigrant Families in One New York Tenement*. New York: HarperCollins, 2010.

A NOTE ON THE AUTHOR

Daniel Duane is the author of the surf memoir *Caught Inside* and the recipient of a 2011 National Magazine Award for "Five Meals Every Man Should Master," an article about cooking with chef Thomas Keller. Duane's food writing has been nominated for a James Beard Award and anthologized in *Best Food Writing 2011.* He collaborated with Alice Waters on the book *Edible Education: A Universal Idea.* His journalism has appeared in *Food & Wine, Bon Appétit,* the *New York Times Magazine, Esquire,* and *GQ,* and he is a contributing editor for *Men's Journal.* Duane lives in San Francisco with his wife, the writer Elizabeth Weil, and their two daughters, Audrey and Hannah.